To my favorite guy!
Thanks for your love &
support.

Love, P. Sherrod

YOUTH BETTER RECKON-EYES

YOUTH BETTER RECKON-EYES

KAWAN SHEPPARD

Rev. date: 08/24/2015

To order additional copies of this book, contact:
Xlibris
1-888-795-4274
www.Xlibris.com
Orders@Xlibris.com
714621

CONTENTS

ACKNOWLEDGMENTS

Throughout my life, I have been blessed to meet and know many influential people. Two of the people who have had the most impact on my life are my parents, Leon and Patricia Sheppard. I have the utmost respect and undying love for my mom and dad. Lavonne Evans, Dionne Robins, and Leonard Sheppard—my sisters and brother—were also great encouragement for me along the way. I love you all from the bottom of my heart.

My godparents, Walter and Gwendolyn Autrey, I love you both. To all my special babies, my nieces and nephews: DaMario Sheppard, Juanice Evans, Raymond Evans, TreNique Walker, Andre and Amir Robins, and JayVon Evans, Auntie loves you all. To all my family, thank you all for your support.

To my pastor whom I was raised under, Elder David Parker, and Dr. Ada, who never changed with the world, thank you for teaching me the importance of true holiness. My present pastor who has spoken into my life and been such a blessing, he and his wife, Elders James and Michelle Davis, I love you both, and thank you for bringing the Word! Special thanks to the Zion Apostolic family and New Spirit Akron campus, who prayed with and for me. My favorite teacher, Mrs. Bessie Brown, and her family, who always believed in me, thank you, and I know that a mind is a terrible thing to waste!

In my life, I was privileged to have close friends and family who believed in my dreams, and I thank you all, Min. Crystal Darnell, Min. Toni Dorazio, Min. Michael Williams, Min. Shiloh Johnson, Pastor Henry Brunson, Bishop Albert Cooper, Pastor Paulette Taylor, Pastor Adam Giles, Pastor Jerome Parker, Judge Randolph Baxter, Lynette

McNair, Arthaniel Womble, MenYon Thomas, Juan "Jay" Evans, Janice Robinson, Brian Johnson, and my best friend in the world, Freece Cooper, I love you so much. Last but not least, my aunts Sheila Thomas and Tonya Essick. Thank you, Aunt Tonya, for your love and friendship throughout the years. To Aunt Sheila, who took the time to help me through the beginning process of getting my dream off the ground, thanks for everything!

MEMORIES

In loving memory of the special people who had to let go of this world to enter into their eternal rest: Dionne Sheppard Robins, I love and miss you, and you're always in my heart; Donald Thomas, the most energetic uncle in the world; my grandparents Luther and Rosa Thomas, who showed so much courage in their last days; V. Grant, M. McNair Walker, D. Brunson, R. Varner and L. Austin, you'll all forever be in my thoughts.

PROLOGUE

This book was written to inspire the youth today. You can be cool and accepted in the world, but the only true acceptance is by God. You will learn through reading this book that God has already done His part. He has blessed, healed, delivered, and called His chosen ones. It's time for us, as the children of God, to step into our season of fullness.

I pray, in your reading, that something will connect with your spirit and help you view each chapter from both sides and see whose point of view makes the most sense and which one has the best long-term-benefit package for your life. These eye-catching titles are for enjoyment and thoughts to ponder.

Many things are repeated throughout the chapters to bring to the attention of the readers that sex, lies, parties, and drugs are just not worth it. Worldly pleasures are temporary and won't sustain you in these last and evil days that are rapidly approaching. God is speaking, but are you able to hear what thus saith the Lord? Please keep your hearts and minds open and allow the Spirit to minister to you.

CHAPTER 1

First Period

In school, you determine the order of your classes by the period you're assigned to go. First period would be the first class, second the next, and you continue on. Sometimes it will be nice to sit and think about what we put first in our personal lives. We come and go every day, taking for granted the many blessings that God has placed in our paths. We usually put so many more things before God, and we are skipping the fact that money, homework, association, jobs, or anything else shouldn't be first. God should be first, period!

Teach Me to Walk. I Got You, Babe

There are many young adults who know what living a saved life is all about, but still there are many who don't. The church isn't having problems getting young people to church, but they're having a hard time keeping them in church after they come. Young newly born-again Christians, also referred to as babes in Christ (1 Pet. 2:2), think that church is just another hang out spot until they mature and understand, it's one of the most important places they will ever go. Church shouldn't be taken lightly; it can change your entire life from just one visit.

We're living in a day when young people are going from church to church because they are young, immature, and most of the time, not patient long enough to be taught anything. Babes don't understand why there are things they can't do yet or positions they can't hold in the church, and then they want to leave. Too many young people want to lead the praise team, take over the youth ministries, and get up and start preaching overnight. We don't go to church for positions, except to get in position to hear from God.

For some reason, babes want to go run the church because somebody told them it was a call on their life. When they aren't appointed positions fast enough then they uproot from where they were, a place where they could grow to church hopping. A lot of times, babes find the singing and praising to by hype, and they sleep on the word. When babes get born again, they find out the attacks start immediately and now realize church can't be just about good music and dancing. Now they're left wondering what's next. I need help!

When a baby is born in the family, the newborn child doesn't have the ability to do too much on their own; it's the same way when you're a babe in Christ. Newborn babies, if you watch them, now they are holding their heads up and bottles earlier on their own. Even though they are becoming independent sooner, they still need their food prepared, as well as other everyday task done for them. Likewise you still need the Word fed to you even if you are anointed. You'll go through hard times when you don't know what to do and still need encouragement to stay in the family.

Just as a flower sits in the light and needs water in order to grow and have its roots go deep, so should a babe in Christ. You should be under a leader who is planting more seeds into you, showering you with the Word of God, and fertilizing you for proper growth. You should have a church home under leadership whose roots are deep. You need to commit to prayer and Bible study weekly and stay in the light for a while. Lastly, allow your Shepherd to hold you until you grow stronger.

One thing amazing about God is you could be sitting in the balcony of a mega church, but if God has need of you, He will someway; somehow have you in the right place at the right time. You will never have to try to make yourself known, like so many are doing today. God has his own spotlight when it's your time to shine.

God has to make sure you are able to withstand the different conditions He sends for you to weather. If you can make it through the seasons, as you get stronger, He will allow you to begin budding into a beautiful flower, one He can plant somewhere and use for His glory. God would never pluck you out the ground before you're ready. He would not have you make a fool of yourself people do that to themselves by uprooting and moving on their own too soon. In your season, He will pick you to handle more responsibilities in the kingdom. 1 Peter 5:6 says, "Humble yourself therefore under the mighty hand of God, that He may exalt you in due season."

In school, you stay in numeric order, going from grade, middle, to high school. In church, there is still order. You're not going to go from the nursery to the pulpit. We understand that God does and can use whom He pleases and whenever He chooses, but God is a god of order. Even His exceptions are in order.

You might have heard the saying, "You have to crawl before you can walk." This even applies in the kingdom. When a babe is learning to walk, they fall over and over again. So many babes don't know what to do when they hit the ground a few times. Some won't get back up because they don't have enough fertilization (faith) and aren't wise enough to go to God. Another cause of babes falling is when they don't have enough stored food (the Word). The absence of this makes them very weak.

As a babe, your faith hasn't been tried in the fire yet, and we know without faith, God can't be pleased. When you were a baby and fell, not knowing you were using faith, you believed if you tried one more time to stand up and take one more step, you'll be walking. In Christ, we have to be liked that. As a new babe, you will make mistakes, sometimes the same one over and over, but you must get back up. You might even spit up food, which is the Word that you don't want to hear. You'll cry if you want something bad enough, or if you don't get your way, you'll even be chastised. Hebrew 12:6 says, "Whom the Lord loveth He chasteneth, and scourged every son He receive."

You'll have good and bad days. You'll be happy and sad at times. You'll have days when you'll rebel and days when you're obedient. You must get up, and when you feel like you can't walk, crawl. God will never leave you or forsake you.

Allow God to elevate you, and you'll be sure to stand. You might be asking, "How do I walk?" My only advice would be to walk by faith and not by sight. Let God take His time to mold you into who He wants you to be, get in some good soil because only God knows your full growth potential. He'll have you ready in your season, He'll lead if you follow, He'll catch you if you fall, and He'll keep you if you want to be kept! Don't forget, God's got you, babe.

I Need a Feeling! Fill Me Up, God!

Recently I discovered I had a lot of teeth that needed to be filled. Before the dentist could do any work on me, first he had to examine my mouth and take x-rays. After taking a picture and identifying which teeth were good and bad, he then went ahead with the cleaning process. My next appointment was when he worked on my teeth that needed to be repaired, starting with the ones in the worse condition.

I compare my process with my dentist to the process we go through with God. First, you acknowledge you're hurting and you need Him then call Him up in prayer. Next, you examine the situation you're facing, use faith, and see yourself coming out. You get rid of the bad choices, people, and mind-sets. Humble yourself, and clean up your act. When going through God, you must recognize that your feelings might get hurt and there are holes that aren't meant to be filled, some things must be totally extracted.

Many times our emotions play a major role in what we go through and how we come out. In my younger years when I was a babe in Christ, I would always look around and wonder why everyone was so excited, jumping and shouting. I would leave the service, questioning if I was truly saved. My praise wasn't like everyone else's. I felt weird and out of place. In church, we get caught up in our emotions.

I would leave church and go home, asking for my own praise. Still not feeling like the Lord was moving over me like He was with others, I felt hesitant to praise and worship. I would be so focused on what didn't happen during praise service that when the Word came forth, I was distracted by my thoughts. I wanted to cry, jump, scream, and run around the church too. God had to show me through my prayer life that He was already surrounding me with His presence. He tells us to worship Him in spirit and truth (1 Sam. 12:24). All I had to do was be myself in Christ, and He gave me my own praise. I found out through maturing in Christ that He moves and touches people differently.

When I first got saved, I was just graduating from high school, and not too much was going on in my life. I would tell the Lord how thankful I was for my parents, my siblings, my life, my health, and my strength. After praying this for months, I thought, *How elementary*. Not only was my worship experience questionable but now my prayer life! To make matters worse, I would really feel lost once the pastor would say, "Remember how God snatched you out the crack house?" Or he would say, "Remember how God kept your mind when you almost lost it?"

I started to wonder how the Lord could send me to help others and I never went through anything. I began feeling like God couldn't use me because I didn't have a testimony. When I really began to press harder, I began to feel Him. The more I worshipped Him and loved on Him, the more He would manifest Himself to me. His presence would sometimes come in tears, and in other times, in clapping or waving my hands. The Lord helped me to see that I didn't have to go through what other kids my age had to endure.

I was already blessed and had every reason to praise Him just as much as anyone else. The fact that I didn't get abused, molested or have parents that were on drugs showed His worthiness. He had given me praise with a bruised-free heart from my childhood. I was looking for a feeling that had already been filled. God, being the great physician that He is, had already extracted my hurts and pain and capped it with praise. He gave me just what I wanted, no condemnation and no remembrance of my sins or my old man. He had created in me a clean heart and renewed the right spirit within me.

Maybe you are the person who has been through all kinds of things in life and you are the opposite. You can't stop praising Him, and you're able to say you watched the hand of God move in your life and remove you out of some crazy situations. Well, keep on praising Him, and He will continue to check up on you if you keep your praise appointments.

We must be like David. In spite of how we feel, we have to make up in our mind that we will bless the Lord at all times (Ps. 34:1). You praise God for who He is, not because of emotions or how you feel. We praise a god who changes not (Mal. 3:6). You may never jump or run around the church, or you might have never went through any drama, but God still demands a praise regardless of how you are feeling. Don't allow your feelings to prevent you from receiving your crown.

So what is the prescription for how you feel? Open your mouth, let God fill it with praise, pull the bad parts out from the roots, and put braces in the crooked areas of your life so when He calls on you, you'll be able to walk straight before Him. God loves you and only wants the best for you, and with everything you have been through or going through now, know that God will order your steps into clean living. Whether you feel Him or not, whether you feel like it or not, keep praising God for who He is because for some reason, I have a feeling everything is going to be all right.

Raise Your Hands If You're Sure.
Keep Them Up Even If You're Not

In your Christian walk, you'll go through dry periods. This time is when you feel like God isn't there and doesn't hear you. You might feel isolated and alone, and some might give up on God. When you keep on doing what you know isn't right in the sight of God and continue to mess up and you feel like you can't give Him praise, this is when you need to pray and ask God for help. When you get to this point, your spirit is so down you go through this stage of not caring and not feeling worthy. This behavior normally results in you continuing in sin instead of repenting!

When you are a child of God—meaning you're saved, filled, and delivered—you can go to your Father because you aren't a slave to sin. "There is no condemnation to them that are in Christ" (Rom. 8:1). With an unsaved person that's not in Christ, they must go to God with a heart of repentance and turn from their god and come into the family of the only true and living God. The key is a heart of repentance, and because God knows the hearts of man, He knows if you mean it or not!

It's so easy for us to give up on God, ourselves, and our dreams when we're not walking in faith. When you are in Christ and have faith, with Christ living on the inside, He will stir you up and give you the strength to go on. God has people in the earth to carry out His plan, and most of the time, it's to benefit someone else! You might not go with the route God set for you, but after not having peace, you'll eventually choose His will. **Until you do what God wants, you will not have peace!** He will still give you freedom of choice the same as He did for Adam and Eve in the garden, Abraham in his sacrifice, and Job when he lost everything and could have cursed God and didn't. He'll let us further punish ourselves or make the choice to do the right thing. No matter what, He still loves us unconditionally. In Romans 8:35, it says, "Who can separate us from the love of Christ?"

While working one day, there was a guy. I asked him if he went to church. He said yes. I told him I could tell because he had such a sweet spirit and was so pleasant to be around. He said, "It's good to know that God still has His hand on me." I smiled. But if you think about it, God is always holding us in His hands. We're the ones that turn our backs and stop seeking His face!

A song that I'm not too thrilled to hear people sing says, "When you've tried everything and everything has failed, try Jesus." We have this mind-set to run to God once everything else fails. Why not go to God because He's God? By going to Him first and being obedient to His Word, nothing will fail. There is no failure in God. God will be your sure thing, as He is for many people, if you trust Him. If He does something for someone else, He can do it for you! So often we look at the length of time or the outcome and judge if God hears us. If God doesn't jump in our timing, we get bent out of shape, but delay doesn't mean denial.

No matter how unsure you are, keep your hands up. He tells us not to lean to our own understanding and acknowledge Him, and He'll direct our paths (Prov. 3:5–6). He's assuring us that we don't have to be sure or understand to lean on Him. At times we want to feel in control of our circumstances. You're not walking in faith until you feel totally dependent on God. God's changes for your life might be uncomfortable, but in the long run, it will be satisfying and fulfilling. You might raise your hands when you're sure, but if you trust God and put your faith in Him, God will help you keep them uplifted even when you're not.

CHAPTER 2

Tardy Bell

The tardy bell is something nobody wants to hear when they're already running behind. On the flip side, there are some people who can't wait for the bell because they're ready to get started. Some of us aren't ready for God to return, w hile others are just getting to the point that they recognize it's about time to get it together. There are others who are allowing their environment to kill them. Which are you? Either way count yourself privileged that God is giving you more time to get the Hell out of your life!

I'm Not Ready! I'll Give You Fifteen

How many times or how frequently do we say, "Lord, I promise I won't do that again"? How many times do you do it again? How much mercy do we expect from God? The Bible talks about a man who was told he was going to die. His name was Hezekiah. When he heard that he was going to die, he turned to pray and asked the Lord to remember how he walked in truth and a perfect heart.

Hezekiah asked the Lord to remember all the good he did. Would you be able to ask the Lord to remember your good works or how you walked in truth? Do you think Hezekiah had time to ask for forgiveness and repent? How many of us would get more from God if we asked, whether it's more years, money, or anything else we asked for? He was noted to have a perfect heart. The Lord told Isaiah to tell Hezekiah He will add fifteen more years to his life. He was saying, "Lord, I'm not ready," and God's response was, "I'll give you fifteen." What an honor when the lifestyle you live is so pleasing to God that when you're at the end of the road, God grants you favor.

There were many times in my life when I should have died or a situation should have come out short, but because of grace, God decided to add more on my behalf. There were times I had deadlines, either for schoolwork, my job, or something that I wasn't prepared for. Unlike Hezekiah I didn't have a spot free past. I prayed and found (undeserved) favor with God. We should keep this story in mind when we need His favor. Walk upright before God while you still have breath so if God came for you, you'll be ready, or get more time.

When God says you lived a pleasing life in His sight, you can feel worthy to ask Him to save you from your death sentence. Many people would say their life has been filled with one battle after another. Some people really want to live upright, but it's a struggle. You want to be greatly used in the ministry, but you can't make it through the test. Everyone is saying, "Lord more of thee and less of me", and that is exactly what is happening, He is doing more and in return He is getting less from us in every area of our lives!

We blame the devil for every hardship when it's not always the devil. The Lord has the final say in everything that a child of God goes through. Job was a good example of the Lord allowing one of His children to go through the fire. God allows things to happen to increase our faith and others' faith in Him. Sometimes we suffer because we're hardheaded. Hezekiah also humbled himself before God. The scripture records him weeping sore before the Lord.

Our attitude when confronted by God has a lot to do with our outcome. How do you respond when God allows the devil to challenge you? Do you walk around mad, treat people bad, or act crazy? God has more for us; He's in the blessing business. We support all these other merchants and never walk through the door of blessings, where we don't have to go broke to get what we want.

Obedience will unlock your storehouse of blessings. Yes, our world should revolve around more than just gym shoes, jewelry, brand-name clothes, video games, nice homes, cars, and the latest technology, but God doesn't mind giving us those things if we give Him what's required of us.

God has so much more to give on such a larger scale, if you walk upright before Him. We don't know when, but we do know we're all going to get this message from God. I would suggest you be ready. God is saying, "I'm returning soon. It might be in five, ten, or fifteen!" Will you be ready to answer when Jesus calls your name? How much more time would you get to prepare yourself? Would God say, "I'll be back" or "Ready or not, here I come"?

Lord, Take Me Out! I'm Ready to Die!

How many requests to the Lord have you heard like this? How many people's prayer is for the Lord to take them out? Only when you are truly ready to die is when you need to pray this. So many times we're asking for things to be placed into our lives rather than praying for ungodly things to be removed. When you get to the point where you're not happy with yourself, nothing can satisfy you, and you're always mad at the world, you'll pray this. When your life is full of confusion, this would be the time to surrender all to Jesus.

I came to my crossroad in life when I discovered that all I was doing was going in circles. I repeated tests and trials that I knew I shouldn't have been going through. All my prayers were all about me. I began to get on my own nerves, begging and feeling like a spoiled little girl. I thought all I had to do was ask Daddy for whatever I wanted, and *bam*! It appears. Not so!

Even though I have always been a giver, sower, and tither, there was a point in my life when I became selfish. Sometimes you have to just die out. God will bless those that He knows will be a blessing to someone else and His kingdom. So many times we want to be blessed—it's for our personal gain or to impress others. It is so important to die to your flesh daily. Your flesh will have you doing things and acting in ways that aren't pleasing to God. I used to be mean during my teenage years because I was fighting so hard to ignore what God wanted for me. I wanted to be like all teenagers and have fun without thinking about the consequences. How many times have you heard that you can't get away with things others can because you know better? I have heard that once or twice before.

Some people have bad attitudes, constantly making smart remarks, always rolling their eyes, all for no reason. I had to pray that the Lord stepped in my life because I didn't want to carry on that way. If you stared in my direction or even spoke to me, I would get mad, more signs that it was time to die. If we would let go of these rebellious spirits that doesn't want to submit to God, the world would be a better place.

We all know that the first thing the enemy does is try to attack our minds. I was a child of God, and I knew better than acting like this, but if you don't die even your ability to think correctly will be compromised. The company you keep is also very important. You can't try to live a saved life hanging out with people who are just living.

I had to disconnect myself from a lot of people. Once I discovered there was nowhere to hide, I died. This spirit I was carrying was so tough I couldn't just drop it. I had to kill it. No, we don't have to act like we're never angry or upset about things, but we're told through the Word, "Be ye angry, and sin not: let not the sun go down upon your wrath. Neither give place to the devil" (Eph. 4:26–27).

We call ourselves Christians, always yelling the blood of Jesus, and don't get along with our blood relatives! All the things we lack in our spiritual walk, we also lack in our physical lives. We don't love our earthly brothers because we don't know our Heavenly Father (God). We hate our neighbors because we never gave the man upstairs a chance (God)! How is your attitude? How is your tone and body language? Are you offending others by what you say and the things you do? "If your hand offends thee," Mark 9:43 says, "cut it off: it is better for thee to enter into life maimed, than having two hands to go to hell, into the fire that never shall be quenched."

So often we feel like our words are the only way to show we have an attitude; even though it is one way, it isn't the only way. Body language is very important. Have you ever asked someone a question, and their mouth answered softly and their body language loud? Gestures, facial expressions, and body movement can sometimes be more harmful than words. We need to be careful as children of God because someone's always watching. We should pay close attention to what we do and say while dealing with others.

James 1:26 says, "If any man among you seem to be religious, and bridled not his tongue, but deceives his own heart, this man's religion is vain." Our Father doesn't want something this minor to be the reason we're held back from major blessings. Thinking about death can be hard, especially when the one dying is you. We should put aside all our old ways, taking on the new man. This is a struggle because our flesh is going to war against our spirit.

Has there ever been a time when you slept on your hand, you wake up and your hand is limp? You move it, and it's still numb, so you shake it. You discover your hand doesn't have any feeling, so you sit and wait until your circulation comes back. That's how young Christians start off. God takes your hand, shakes the bad off: lying, gossip, jealousy, and sometimes the haters—He has to shake them off too! This is an important process that we must go through during our transition.

Some doctors and scientists believe there's going to be a disease that kills the world; I believe that disease is hatred. As 1 John 4:8 says, "He who does not love does not know God, for God is love." So many claim to know God and really don't because they don't love themselves. Love was one of the greatest messages God tried to instill in us, even from Him giving His only begotten Son because He so loved the world.

When you die in the natural, you must make proper arrangements. It's the same in a spiritual death. You make an announcement confessing you're a changed person and the old you is deceased, pick your wardrobe out of things you should and shouldn't be wearing as a child of God, put on the garment of praise and worship, lastly get a good casket and burial plan. We don't want anything that can't keep the old man restrained for good. Have a gathering for your family and friends, some you'll have to separate from and some you can keep, but you must sort everything out before you begin your service for Christ! Some won't understand why and others will, but God will help them to move on because He is a comforter.

Eventually once your service starts, others won't have a choice but to go along with the program! Let everyone know there isn't a need for a final viewing because you're already changed, so they won't see the old you they knew anyway! Are you willing to die for Christ? After all, He died for you! It's time to decide if you're going to die to self and live for Christ or just be in this world as another dead man walking. Choose ye this day!

007, Once an Assignment, Now an Assassin

There are things in our lives that murder our spirits. Some things in life were assigned to you, and others were created by you. When we allow God's work in our lives to sit in an inactive status, it opens up so many avenues for a murder to take place. Our physical bodies isn't the death, but our spirit, our joy, our drive, and our witness, they're some of the first to be taken out.

Certain people are placed in our lives not for us to hang out with or date, but for us to be an example and for them to see how a delivered young person is supposed to live. You're like their spiritual boot camp trainer. Schoolteachers were known to leave a note when they were going to be absent to the substitute. They would let them know that if they needed any help, ask their star student. Even though the teacher knew that all the kids were the same age and were capable of acting up, they just trusted they could depend on that one student.

That scenario is kind of like how God is with us. He makes us over, shapes us, and then sends us out to people who need some help or backup. Not saying you don't have your own devils, God just doesn't expect you to be the one showing out when you know who He is.

Sometimes life gets so rough you feel like you're being set up for a slow murder. The enemy will wait until you get your instructions for your new assignment and start moving in on you. As soon as you step in war territory, he makes the battle more intense. God sends you your assignment, and Satan sends the opposite sex to seduce you. Satan takes your focus off your once assignment to your now assassin. When our troops get word that they have to go to war, it starts off as their assignment. Some of them lose their lives and are taken out by the enemy, which then becomes their assassin. Our objective going in is to defeat, and sometimes the enemy's plans murder us. The scripture tells us to "pray without ceasing" (1 Thess. 5:17).

The enemy is always waiting for you outside the camp to catch you without your weapon, and sometimes he is in the camp. I often wonder why so many of God's children who should have influence are the main ones being influenced. You're the one with the gift being wrapped around the devil's finger.

Grounds that used to be familiar are now foreign to you. Have you ever been used to going somewhere the same way, and one day you see a detour sign? Now you have to go a new way. You're still in a familiar area yet unfamiliar territory. Satan does a sneak attack once he notice you're directions has you confused. When the detours has you turned around and off track the enemy closes in on you. He makes you feel unworthy so you don't tell the General (God) that the enemy is defeating you. Now you won't go to church because you feel like you're defeated in God's eyes too, even when God told you from the start that you're more than a conqueror.

The sad thing is now we have more young people taking their own lives, committing suicide before the enemy can assail them. Your instructions told you to suit up with the whole armor of God because we don't wrestle against flesh and blood (Eph. 6:12) but you're still trying to look like the enemy. Maybe this is you, it was once me. God will pick you up and dust you off if you "therefore endure hardness, as a good soldier of Jesus Christ" (2 Tim. 2:3). Take charge of the territory God has entrusted you with. Don't let the enemy take you out while you're on your assignment. Get out there, and do what God sent you to do. Witness, recruit, and restore, and you will get your reward! God has a medal of honor waiting for you! Don't give up, soldier. You already have the victory.

Get the Hell Out of Your Life

Growing up in a small-sized church, we were all like family. We had fashion shows, plays, played wholesome games, and had good ole church. There was praise and worship, one offering, a Word from God, altar call, and if the Spirit didn't say otherwise, we were going home.

Church was a place where the sinner could go get delivered and get on the right track. Saints would come hug you warmly and speak life into you. Church used to be an anointed atmosphere. The church mothers were examples and role models. They were known to correct the younger girls and show the older ones how to act and dress like ladies.

When I was younger, church was a place where you could go drop off your burdens without your business being spread around. It was a place where you could talk to your spiritual father and get godly council. Nowadays there's so much going on in the church it's a shame. We are allowing people to stay in these pulpits, knowing they aren't trying to live right. There isn't any conviction or power in the messages today because it's not coming from God. Now it's to the point that preachers are teaching us that if you keep sinning, it's okay; the Lord will forgive you, so people aren't making any effort to change. Now our young folks are continuing in sin and believing they have a lifetime to get it together!

One thing about God is that He is forgiving, but at the same time, He tells us we aren't supposed to be slaves to sin. With that said, if you are doing things and putting yourself in predicaments to sin, then that is intentional, not accidental. When you do what you want intentionally, it becomes iniquity. In Luke 6:46, God ask why do you call me Lord, Lord and do not do what I say?

People try to use the famous I-got-tricked role when it comes to God. Being tricked is when you don't know, or can't see it coming at you, or when a fast one is pulled on you. Going places we have no business, going out with the wrong people, dating someone you know isn't trying to live a saved life, or just not willing to line up with the Word of God is not being tricked!

Sinners feel no heat from their sinful ways because there is so much confusion in the church, and the only thing church has time to discuss in detail is the tithes and offerings! Forget explaining communion being symbolic of God's body and His blood! People living in sin are just going through a prayer having sinful things lined up for the rest of the day and are still partaking in communion! Maybe this is the reason why so many are sick among us!

The lost soul leaves just as lost because nobody takes the time to witness to them anymore. What happens next? They figure church is no different than anywhere else they attend, so they don't go looking to be delivered. They go out of habit and to be entertained!

A movie named the *Passion of the Christ* had many people around the world in tears. For some reason, reading about the crucifixion in the Bible wasn't real enough, so once they had more of a visual, it made it more emotional. People cried and thought about it within the time frame of the movie and the walk back to their car. It still wasn't enough to stop their out-of-control sins, and I didn't believe it would when people can go to a church that is teaching truth week after week and still practice sin!

Every time you and I sin, we put Jesus back on the cross. We put more nails in His hands and feet, and we pierce His side. When we disobey Him, it's like spitting in His face again. If Jesus was depending on us, His wounds would have never healed!

Yes, at times, certain things and problems we face do get hard and frustrating. In 1 Corinthians 10:13, scripture says, "There hath no temptation taken you but such as is common to man: but God is faithful, who will not suffer you to be tempted above that ye are able; but will with temptation also make a way to escape, that you may be able to bear it." How much more can God tell us? He knows what we as young adults go through, but it's nothing nobody else hasn't ever gone through. So just stand, wait on Him, and look for your way out. It's going to come, and you'll be able to handle it, so don't worry. What an awesome God! Once you get the Word in your heart and speak the Word to your situations, the more you practice, the easier it will become, and the better off you'll be.

We must be like David. He said, "Thy word have I hid in mine heart, that I may not sin against thee." God is looking for some young people who will keep it real. Not the real of today because saying what you want in the pulpit, dancing like you're in the club, and all the other foolishness isn't real or smart just real crazy! He is looking for young people to be holy because He is holy! We have been hearing God is coming back for many years, and just because He hasn't come yet, it doesn't mean He's not coming. He's just giving you more time to get the hell out of your life!

CHAPTER 3

Lunch Hour

No matter where you are, most people can hang around anywhere once they make it to their lunch hour. At school or work, once it's time to eat, everything is okay. Some people hang with friends; others are at home watching talk shows or soaps. But in most cases, people are getting some type of food. Whatever you're doing during your lunch hour, make sure it's healthy for you.

Wanna Be Healthier? Eat More Fruit!

We live in an economy where every other person is overweight. There is so much obesity going on, especially with our children. Experts are urging people to stay away from fast food and junk food and to eat healthier. They are encouraging us to stay home and prepare home-cooked dinners for our families. If you could afford to, they really prefer that you eat organic foods and fruits. Fitness experts are pushing exercise to become a daily regimen.

When you turn on the television, there you'll hear the doctors telling you that if you want to be healthier, you need to lose weight, and they have the perfect pill that will guarantee thirty pounds in thirty days. In bookstores, they have day-by-day instructionals on what to eat and the serving sizes. Being healthy, there are a million ways to do it, but still millions are overweight. God tells us that the best formula for being healthy isn't the low-carb diet, Weight Watchers, South Beach, Jenny Craig, or Atkins diet plans, but His plan. God recommends that for us to be healthy, we have to eat more fruit—the fruit of the spirit, love, joy, peace, long-suffering, gentleness, goodness, faith, meekness, and temperance.

So many people are carrying so much extra weight because they have so much hate in them. You can't say you're saved when you are being rude and bitter all the time. My question is, what are you saved from? I know people who are up one day speaking and talking nice, and by the next day they developed an attitude, acting as if they never knew you. This isn't the behavior of a Christian. This is more of a bipolar than Christ-like behavior. God gave us the fruit of love, which is easier to do than being hateful; don't forget we serve a god who is love.

Joy is the next fruit. People aren't eating it because their spirits are down, and they're constantly allowing Satan to whisper negativity in their ear. "The joy of the Lord is your strength" (Neh. 8:10). There are times when we want to lean on the world and not the Word for our strength. We constantly try to use our own strength to bench-press against the enemy. You'll never win going against Satan alone in competition without God. Peace is a fruit that many Christians act as if they're allergic to. God tells us He'll keep us in perfect peace "whose mind is stayed on thee" (Isa. 26:3). People have so much chaos in their lives and keep so much mess going on that they don't have peace of mind. This is because they won't digest peace on a regular basis.

Young folks don't exercise long-suffering. We're a want-everything-fast generation. Long-suffering can be like milk—it can do the body good. Patience is the next fruit that carries no weight in our everyday actions. We don't want to wait for anything! The reason so many folks are rough on others, from the youth all the way to the elderly is because we don't have gentleness. This fruit isn't talked about because everyone wants to turn fat into muscle to appear tough. They want to appear this way so when others look at them, people won't think they're soft or weak. Gentleness is harder for men to digest than women because young men are taught they will be punks if they show any signs of sensitivity. Young men grow up not knowing they can show emotions and still be a man.

David said, "Surely goodness and mercy shall follow me all the days of my life, and I will dwell in the house of the Lord forever" (Ps. 23:6). *Goodness* is the "state or quality of being good," "excellence," or "merits worth." You can't buy this fruit from but one vendor: God. People don't honor their word anymore. They don't care what others think about their character or their actions. When you can't be trusted or your name doesn't hold weight, that is bad. Scripture teaches us that "a good name is rather to be chosen than great riches, and loving favour rather than silver and gold" (Prov. 22:1).

Another fruit not being eaten that will help a lot is faith. Faith is the seventh fruit mentioned in the passage, and seven is the number of completion; you aren't complete in God until you have faith. I could stop naming healthy fruit with faith; this is the key to living whole. By faith, you must believe that God and Jesus are one. By faith, you must also put confidence in someone you've never seen and be assured in your spirit that you're living solely for Him so you can rest in Him for eternity.

Faith is the brain food of all the fruit. When it's properly eaten, it will build you up with boldness and confidence to keep on going. You won't need a money-back guarantee once you get faith. You'll lose the weight of the world, your body will start to develop, and you'll definitely pick up muscle or power in the areas where you are struggling.

God adds meekness to the group, which goes hand-in-hand with long-suffering. They both have to do with patience and waiting. The unique thing about meekness is that you eat this like a banana—you peel it down. You are showing signs of humility. Meekness is peeling off pride and high-minded ways and becoming submissive or humble. In Christ, you must remember there is but one who is high and sits on the throne, and that is God.

The world's baskets are so full of natural fruits and not enough spiritual fruit. They have too many preservatives, and now the church is being overwhelmed with more basket-case saints than ever before.

Christians are doing like the farmers, not letting their fruit grow all the way until it's ready to be picked, because of the lack of patience and greed, we are forced to eat partially prepared foods, causing people to be undernourished naturally and spiritually.

Then there is temperance. Some Christians only have the first part: tempers! This is moderation or self-restraint. It seems to be harder for ladies, but guys have their issues too. Women are out shopping when they can't afford to, buying shoes, expensive purses, and clothes. Ladies feel like they have to buy makeup, get their hair and nails done every two weeks and it's not in their budget, going places borrowing your bill, school, and sometimes tithes and offering just to impress others.

We all have been there. Guys have some of these habits, including having car fetishes, wanting all the latest electronics, and wanting to buy things to impress others, knowing they don't have the money. Most people don't have balance in their lives. They overdo it on what they like and fall short on what they need. Temperance will prevent you from trying to keep up with others.

No matter if you're a teen or a young adult, eating the right food will make you feel better and live more balanced lives. In our physical bodies, we can't just eat things with fruits in them, like Fruit Roll-Ups, fruit drinks, or Fruit Loops. In order for you to be healthier, you have to eat more fruit of the Spirit.

One Life to Live, Not Another Soap!

While talking with other young adults, they would often inquire what I did in my free time. It seems like once I didn't mention drinking, smoking, and clubbing, they would automatically assume that my life was boring! The next statement that was sure to follow was, "You're too young to not do anything. Life's too short, you better live and enjoy yourself."

For some reason, people think that if you're not involved in the fast life, then you're not living your life to its fullest. It amazes me how much people of the world are like characters from the soap operas. They are totally serious about their roles whether it's of good or bad character, they always put on a good show, they're always confused as to what's going on around them, and it's episode after episode in their lives. Worldly people always feel that if it's not their way of kicking it, then you're not having a good time.

I found out there's a lot of alternative things you can do other than party. If you are mentally confused or the devil has blinders on you, it would be hard for you to see any other way. Living saved and young doesn't have to be hard or boring, but when Satan has you bound, he will keep you ignorant of all the benefits of being saved. Many young people have allowed the world and its deceitful tactics to brainwash them to the extent they can't conceive God's way as being the only way.

Satan's fun is just for a season. When you become aware that only what you do for Christ will last, everything in the world and of the world won't look so grand after all. Getting down and living it up are two ways you can look at it. Getting down (going down), as the world views it, includes parties and clubs; vices, profanity, theft and murder. These are the things the world thinks is cool.

The lifestyles mentioned are empty and low-life living. You will still find yourself on the search for true fulfillment. Living it up (to go up) is praying, fasting, having a relationship with God, worshipping, giving, and sacrificing fleshly desires. These are things that never play out or never get boring, and at the same time, they are developing your character to become more Christ like, while preparing you to live in eternity with Him.

The Word says, "examine yourselves whether ye be in faith; prove your own selves, how that Jesus Christ is in you, except ye be reprobates?

But I trust that ye shall know we are not reprobates" (2 Corinthians 13:5,6). Young people who are on this faith walk must understand that it doesn't take a smart person to live ungodly, but it takes a wise person to live for God.

When I read the story of Samuel and Saul and how God told Saul to kill everything but he did what he wanted to and disobeyed God, this showed Saul wasn't wise! The Lord said to Samuel, "It repenteth Him that He set up Saul to be king: for he is turned back from following me, and hath not performed my commandments" (1 Sam. 15:11). The Lord tells us we're rebelling when we disobey and aren't living according to the Word. The Bible says that rebellion is as the spirit of witchcraft (1 Sam. 15:23).

God promises us that blessings shall overtake us if we obey the Word and keep His commandments. Who wouldn't want to be blessed by God to the point that His blessings overtake them? Only God knows what our future holds. Because we don't know the great things He has in store for us, it seems to be no big deal. We continue to kick it and further delay our promised inheritance from our Father. It makes me think of the saying, "You never miss what you never had."

Young people aren't taking time to read the Word to know what they're entitled to once they say yes to God's will! A lot of saved people are taking on fights that aren't theirs. Many aren't getting proper rest because of stress, anxiety, and worry. You would think that after this happens over and over, you would catch on to that one life you have to live, you're spending most of your time in General Hospital from mental breakdowns when God wants to give you breakthroughs.

God is saying, "All my children are growing up having problems," and this is why there are so many Christian SSI (saved, struggling, and ignorant) recipients in the church. The church is allowing doctors to tell us our youth has ADD, ADHD, and learning disorders. Young people need to be on the altar until they are free from these busy spirits and generational curses. Christians should be exercising the power on the inside of them until they see a change.

With the situations that are challenging our country as the world turns, look for things to get worse. Young people, now is not the time to be like Saul disobeying God. You need to be girded, ready to fight this war. God raised you up for this purpose and time. You were raised up to fight and should be fighting to be raised. We don't have time to be the young and the restless. We have work to do. God made us the bold and beautiful generation. We were put on this earth during this time to be guiding lights to those that are lost.

Young people, it is time out for playing church and acting saved and really get delivered! You should be letting other young people tune in to you living holy because the things the youth is faced with now is reality and not just another soap.

Friends, a Love-Hate Relationship

Jesus walked throughout the cities when He went to teach. He had the twelve disciples with Him even though they weren't all real friends. Wherever He went, they followed; whatever He told them to do, they did. A lot of people have had friends they were so tight with that you would have thought they were shadows. When you see one, you see them both. You always had one friend that knew you better than anyone, the one who held the key to your every intimate secret. There are some people who you have allowed access to your virtual reality.

Jesus went through a betrayal by one of his so-called friends and was denied by another. Judas hung out with Jesus, ate with Him, and saw Jesus perform miracles. For the most part, he could have been viewed as a friend in the beginning but he ended up being an enemy.

I'm sure we've all heard the saying, "Keep your friends close and your enemies closer." You'll have people in your circle whose intentions are good, but they will sell you out because they don't have any loyalty. Peter claimed he wouldn't deny Jesus. Not once, twice, but three times he did just that: he denied Jesus. Judas, on the other hand, outright sold Jesus out for only thirty pieces of silver. He played Jesus like so-called friends play some of us—real cheap.

Peter thought he had Jesus back, but when the going got rough, Peter got going. Peter is kind of like the so-called friend who will talk about fighting with you and get you pumped up, and when the actual fight goes down, they're nowhere to be found. They want to be in your corner, but they just don't have the courage to live up to what they agreed to.

I have had to stop hanging with people because I loved them as a person but hated things about them. I would enjoy being around them until they were jealous when all the attention wasn't on them. I liked talking to them until they could never compliment others and were always being negative. They were cool to play sports with, but I came to the end of the rope with them being on my team.

Everyone has their own definition of what a friend is. Your enemies don't always have to be outside of your circle, sometimes you live with them. Satan will use your own parents against you if they're not saved and delivered. Have you ever heard someone's parents say to them, "If you're going to drink and smoke, do it with me, therefore I know it's all good"? Yes, they might say they love you, but they are allowing Satan to use them to hate on you, your life, your dreams, and your future.

Judas really thought he was slick. Girls probably can understand him a little better than guys. Have you ever had a so-called friend who had a friend that you didn't care for? What the girl would do is come up with the perfect script and call you up on three-way while the other girl you didn't care for was quiet. The instigator is asking why you don't like her and who said what. She's finding out all the details and confirming all your answers so the next time you see the other girl, she's ready to fight. Judas had his plans set up too. The Bible says in Mark 14 that Judas sought how he might conveniently betray him.

Judas must have forgotten that God knows all, even our thoughts before we think them, so we can't pull any fast ones over on Him. Jesus said to them, "Verily, verily I say unto you, that one of you shall betray me" (Matt. 26:21). Judas even asked if it was him. One thing I don't like is phony people. People like Judas will smile in your face, sit and eat with you, and talk to you, all the while they're trying to take you out. God, being God, still allowed him to sit and eat the last supper with the rest of the disciples.

Throughout the Bible, God displayed a calm nature about Himself because He's so much higher and wiser than we are. Most of us would have gone off as soon as we found out what Judas was doing, but God wasn't surprised. We shouldn't be surprised either when we are treated wrong, betrayed, or set up by Satan. Just as God promised us He would make our enemies our footstool in Matthew 22:44, we must learn to step back and allow God to repay those who betray us.

The story goes on to say how Judas confessed his wrongs, gave back the silver, and hung himself. Every time you put situations, flesh, and feelings before God, you must confess, you always end up hanging yourself. God, being so full of love, was hated enough to be betrayed. Are you greater than your master? Matthew 10:22 says, "And ye shall be hated of all men for my names sake: but he that endureth to the end shall be saved."

We often ignore the fact that God is the only one who promises to never leave us and really doesn't. Yet and still, we will ignore His promises over boyfriends, girlfriends, or plain ole friends. When you discover that God is a friend who sticks closer than a brother and He wants more for you than you can think to want for yourself, then you will agree that in life you'll run into many so-called friends and will experience many love-hate relationships because can't nobody do you like Jesus. God is the only faithful one who knows how to love you because He's not the kind of friend who wants to hate on you. Check the crowds around you, the people in your circle, and ask yourself, am I a friend of God's?

CHAPTER 4

Picture Day

Every school year, this day rolls around. The classes that are most excited about pictures are the elementary kids and the seniors. For the underclass group, it's a new experience. For the senior class, they are just happy about getting a portfolio full of pictures of them at their best. In the next few pages, you will read that it does matter how you look, and even though many will try to deceive you with their I-don't-care attitude, you better make sure your first shot comes out right because you might not get any retakes. So get your look together, or picture God returning and you being left behind.

How Do I Look?

Most people look in the mirror and wonder if their look is just right before going to their favorite hangout, whether it be to the mall on the weekends or social organizations they're involved in. Most people will check themselves out from head to toe before leaving home. A lot of the times, if it's a special occasion, people begin preparing for it days, weeks, and sometimes, months in advance. For example, you might not have an outfit in your closet that meets your expectations for the place you're going, so you'll run out to the store and purchase everything you need so you'll look good when you leave the house. When the world says, "Don't come looking any kind of way," they mean it, so you listen. You'll go get your hair, nails, and toes done; buy jewelry, outfits, hats, shoes; and even rent a vehicle for the event.

Everywhere you go, there is a dress code. Stores have signs that say, "No shoes, no shirts, no service," and clubs will have proper dress required, with signs that say, "No tennis shoes, hoodies, or jeans." If you're not wearing the correct attire, you don't get in! Going to concerts, you get all dressed up to sit in a dark, hot, crowded, sweaty-smelling theater or stadium where you're barely seen. Why then when we go to the heavenly courts before the king, do we start lowering the standards for how we look? Then we use the "come as you are" policy. To me, "Come as you are" means if you're an alcoholic, drug addict, or murderer, come to Him, He can and will deliver. It doesn't mean for you to put on your short tight skirts and jeans, hot pants, flip flops, tight slacks, muscle shirts, jogging pants, or throwbacks and go to church. You are going to a sacred sanctuary where the presence of God dwells! Let's take it a step further a lot of jobs you can't dress any way you like and show your tattoo's or you get sent home, so why would you use God's house as a showcase for something He doesn't want on your body in the first place?

No other place lowers their standards or compromises with people, except when it comes to the church. The church will allow anything and everything, knowing people have or get access to the proper attires when they have to, but they don't at church because there aren't any standards in the house of God. You might remember when people used to point out women in the church from their long dresses, gym shoes, and no makeup on their faces. Church picnics and skating parties, it didn't matter; the women would have skirts down to their ankles.

Now you'll do good if you can go into a church and pick out who the pastor's wife is! We don't have to look old-fashioned or dry, but you should look holy! Saved young men and women should have a unique style and look like a child of God. After all, our father is a king. You can tell when people are wealthy with class by their appearance and how they carry themselves. Classy people don't look and behave certain ways. They don't have tight, short clothes on; loud, wild, with weird colors in their hair; crazy styles, huge earrings, tongue rings, and tattoos. These aren't holy appearances or classy, and we should be in a class of our own.

We like to use the scripture 1 Samuel 16:7, when the Lord said to Samuel, "Look not on his countenance, or the height of his stature; because I have refused him: for the Lord seeth not as man seeth; for man looketh on the outward appearance, but God looketh on the heart." This scripture is one of many that we want to use for coming any way. In this passage, He was referring to his facial expression, the look on his face, and his height and stature. He didn't mention anything to make us believe his apparel was included. If you read 1 Thessalonians 5:22, it says, "Abstain from all appearance of evil," which means the worldly look and doing worldly things.

You might say everyone doesn't have church clothes. This is true. Everyone also doesn't have club, formal, concert, and other clothing either. What do you do? Go buy, borrow, or wear the best thing or most appropriate outfit you can find. Wear the same thing until God blesses or makes a way. I had to do that. I just got a plain black skirt and changed my shirts. I did this until I could afford something else. Just thinking about school dances, proms, homecomings, Twins Days, and other school activities, I knew everyone in my class couldn't afford it. But you know what? They came and were dressed appropriately!

When you attend service, make sure you look presentable before you enter the house of God! You would make sure you looked decent before an earthly judge, a man or woman who had to learn the laws, get certified by man and elected to become honorable judges. Where is the respect when it comes to God, the one who created the law and didn't need approval from anyone to be the judge of the world? How much more respect should He get from us who call ourselves

His children? You should be concerned when you're out here acting and dressing any kind of way, and you say you belong to God.

Before you enter into His courts, you need to evaluate yourself and ask the question, how do I look? We surely don't want to misrepresent our king or His kingdom. Just as you would represent your earthly parents with pride, let's show even more respect and pride when representing our Heavenly Father! How you look going to the house of God does matter. Make sure your gift isn't the only thing that looks good on you!

Wanted Christians: Charges, Theft by Deception

I was involved in a situation where a lady, who claimed to be a Christian, sold me a car that wasn't hers. I found out while trying to do a title transfer that the vehicle was never registered in her name. She wasn't being honest or willing to work with me, so we ended up in court. Knowing she was wrong, she never showed up for the hearing. She knew she didn't have a case, so she figured why should she show up? After going to small claims court, I was then advised to go to the police station and file a criminal report.

The first question asked was, what is the offense? When the officer heard the whole story, he figured he would put theft by deception. She stole and lied in one transaction. Theft is when someone, without permission, takes something that doesn't belong to them by way of deceit.

A lot of Christians are stealing God's time, praises, and money. When we don't pray like we are supposed to and we aren't giving God His praises He's worthy of, that's stealing! When we keep His tithes and offerings, we are robbing God (Mal. 3:8). Who wants to be known in the heavens for robbing God? Our firstfruits are the Lord's; 10 percent of all our earnings go to Him. I hear people say, "God doesn't need our money, and He doesn't get it anyways." God doesn't need anything from us, but He doesn't ever tell us to give it because He needs it. He's trying to set us up to be blessed.

God tells us to seek first the kingdom of God and His righteousness, and all these things shall be added unto us (Matt. 6:33). If you're robbing God, it's actually a double count because you are robbing yourself too. You make things so much harder on yourself by giving God the okay to lock the windows of heaven, that His Word promises to be unlocked when you give (Malachi 3:10).

Deception is when you are misleading people or when you are being deceitful. Deceptive people, also known as liars, are displeasing in God's sight. God hates every false way (Ps. 119:104). Liars have a place in hell. Some people call them small white lies as if they aren't any big deal. In God's sight, there aren't any small or large lies—they are all just lies. Proverbs 12:19 says, "A lying tongue is but for a moment."

We have to watch not only what we say but how we say things. Sometimes we don't come straight out with the whole story, which can be deceitful. You hear about sex being bad all the time, but there are more sins being done by our youth than just having sex. We hear about sex so much you would think that if you didn't have sex, you were okay no matter what else you did. Sex is just one of the many sins we can commit.

A liar is someone you don't hear about nearly as much, but God isn't pleased with liars. If you're a liar or a thief, you're under arrest. You have the right to live holy. Anything you say can and will be used only to uplift the name of Jesus and praise His holy name. You have the right to have a pastor to watch over your soul. If you don't have a church home, one can be appointed to you. If you're not honest, repent, for the kingdom of God is at hand.

Icy Hot, Somebody's Been Gay

I've had the privilege of attending a taping for a local news center where I live. The topic was about men on the down-low. I found this to be interesting, informative, yet scary. I learned that it's not just the men who are in prisons or the men who wear women's clothing that are gay. It's also the hard-core rapper, the popular classmate, the one you work beside, and the athletes. They are everyday people not choosing a God-fearing lifestyle.

Some of these behaviors are from childhood molestations or hurts, but all such behavior is from the spirit of the enemy. A lot of women were introduced to this lifestyle from their party lives. Women are out there getting so drunk and high, and men are taking advantage of them. Girls began involving other girls in their relationships and just allowing curiosity to set in! I believe a lot of the music, videos, movies, and wrong influences encourage such behavior. Some girls feel like this is adding creativity to their sexuality.

God tells us to refrain from sex and "flee fornication. Every sin that a man doeth is without the body; but he that committed fornication sinneth against their own body" (1 Cor. 6:18). Disobeying God is bringing on new dimensions of sins. We are to refrain from foolish talk, filthiness, and being whoremongers and live holy. God warns us to not let man deceive us "because these things cometh the wrath of God upon children of disobedience" (Eph. 5:6). This way of life is perverted, not cute, sexy, or fun. It's totally out of order. You will not see the king or the kingdom doing these things.

First Corinthians 6:9 says, "Know ye not that the unrighteous shall not inherit the kingdom of God? Be not deceived: neither fornicators, nor idolaters, nor effeminate." Let's stop here. Do you know what an effeminate is? The dictionary defines it as "having the qualities associated with women; not characteristics of or befitting a man; unmanly." The translation of scripture says it's a boy kept for homosexual relations with a man, or a male who submits his body to unnatural lewdness.

You might have a parent who has allowed you to be raised looking like everything except a young man, and somehow you became confused by wearing long hair and earrings like girls. Now you've developed female tendencies. It's not right, but you can be delivered. This is the same for females: not wearing ladies' attire and walking around with big jeans hanging off you, with do-rags on your heads, and acting like a man. God wants to change you!

The big picture is, the family portrait isn't the same as before! Now there are two women or two men and then the kids! We tell families with mothers and fathers that are separated that a woman can't raise a boy to be a man, and a man can't raise a girl to be a woman. We go on to say our families need both mom and dad in the house. Now we have men who act like women, trying to raise boys to be men or, even worse, just like them! How can they raise something to be a way they're not? More deception! We always hear the story of Creation in Genesis, about God creating man and woman. Nowhere did He create any two things of the same sex for mating purposes. Sodom and Gomorrah were wiped out because of their contrary and disobedient lifestyles. Recently there have been hurricanes, forest fires, and floods destroying cities. I look at this as a wakeup call. So many nonbelievers found themselves not only looking for a place to live but also a church to worship. God allowed many people another chance to see that no matter who throws the party, He's in control of what goes on here. "God judgeth the righteous, and God is angry with the wicked everyday" (Ps. 7:11). Some found out the wage of sins is death.

People who want everyone to like them will say, "It's okay, God loves us all," when it's not okay. God loves us all, but He won't tolerate the things we do when we're sinning against His Word. We can't tell people it's all right to be gay and vote for gay marriages and gay rights. When God says not to do something, you don't have any rights! We must stand for God's Word because the world isn't. How can you be saved and act like God doesn't have standards?

Any job you work has a handbook to abide by. Christian's handbook is the Bible—all sixty-six books from Genesis to Revelation! These books will let you know what you can and can't do as a child in the kingdom. If I have to live holy to make it to heaven, so do you. If I can't drink, smoke, club, and have sex before marriage, how can you? If God commands one not to get involved in homosexual lifestyles, that goes for everyone! Do you think you would see this perversion in heaven? Would you want to? Walking around rebelling against God in heaven, men acting like women and women acting like men, trying to worship Him! You can get away with that in your church, but God isn't going

to tolerate this in His kingdom. If you don't stop it now, I
you there won't be anyone like you in heaven because you
be there!

When I was younger and knew one of my friends or family members
didn't like someone, I would find myself rolling my eyes at them too.
If we are that dedicated to our friends and family, how much more
loyalty should we have for our Heavenly Father? You weren't born again
to keep confusion down; you're supposed to bring it to the light so it
can be cast down. We can't be more concerned about people's feelings
that we don't consider God's. You have to be careful of the company
you keep. You can't let everyone hang around you. Spirits do transfer!
Young people if you are calling yourself saved you have no business with
a best friend that is gay! You shouldn't even be entertained by them.
This says a lot about your walk with Christ when someone with this
spirit is comfortable around you. Eph.5:11 says have no fellowship with
the unfruitful work of darkness but rather reprove them.

God is calling for true holiness. Many young people reading this
book might have even gone through this or going through it now, living
confused and not understanding what's going on in their homes or
bodies. It doesn't have to continue in your life. Learn the Word of God.

He'll lead you out of your confusion and rub your pains down from
the hot situations you've seen because someone has been gay in your life
and you want the ache to stop here. He'll do it for you. He's not a god
that can't be touched by our infirmities. This is a pain that over-the-
counter drugs can't cure because they aren't strong enough. It's going
to take a deeper penetration so the curse can be broken.

God isn't pleased with our nation, and it's time to make a change.
Stand up for righteous living. Same-sex relationships and marriages
aren't right, no matter who votes it in. You might be gay or know
someone who has been gay, know this one thing: hell isn't icy—it's hot!

CHAPTER 5

Book Reports

Sometimes we get caught up in our studies from school, working, and our personal lives. We tend to settle or lower our standards and sometimes not think about what the real book reports, which is the Bible. Read and learn what God's book reports on life and the issues you face day to day.

Give Him Something He Can Feel.
When Was Your Last Intimate Encounter?

The carnal mind will take this topic and assume I'm talking about sex, but I'm not. I'm curious to know when you had your last intimate encounter with God, not man. The first person who was intimate with God that came to mind was the lady with the issue of blood. She had some kind of faith. When all odds were against her, she continued to press on.

This woman pushed through the crowds of people with her issue. Some people would have seen the crowd and would have said, "They got me messed up. I'll just catch up with Jesus later!" Some would have let their miracle walk right past them like we do every day, waiting on later. This lady must have said in her mind, *Enough is enough. I'm going to get rid of this issue once and for all because I'm tired of this following me year after year!*

Many times we go through things for long periods at a time, but when we get to the point of being fed up, we turn and run from Jesus instead of pressing through, running to Jesus. She was desperate to give Him something He could feel. In spite of the circumstances, she still pressed on. With all the odds of being sick, being a woman, and having to push through the crowd and His disciples, she pressed on anyhow, saying, "If I could just touch the hem of his garment, I will be made whole."

"Death and life are in the power of the tongue" (Prov. 18:21). She spoke life to her problem and declared her healing. She could have said, "I might be made whole." Her faith was so sure she had no doubt that just a touch would suffice. When she got to Him, her faith moved God so much that He stopped and wanted to know who just touched Him. How often does your name come up when God asks, "Who just touched me?" The woman stepped forth and told the Lord it was her. After all, His disciples didn't know who touched Him! This lady received her healing because He hadn't seen any greater faith. Jesus met her needs not just because she touched Him, but because in her heart, she believed. God's Word says we can move mountains if we can only believe. We must press on and get in God's face not just with our faith for our problems to be solved but also with our praise to help us through them! There are people and things in our lives we have more faith in than God. Our transportation, teachers, significant others, jobs, and even our pastors, just to name a few. Of all the things we should be believing God for we're trusting in man as if they are going to help us, get us where we need to go, love us, treat us right, and always be there for us. There is no sure thing in this world but God and His Word. I love the words to the song that says, "Don't wait till midnight." We wait until the last hour, the last minute, all the way down to the last second to go to God. After, we've tried everything, and we not only failed but made matters worse. God wants us to have faith in Him to the point where we are totally dependent on Him and He is our first choice. He wants us to feel lost in the crowd without Him, and we should feel like that. The Bible says, "The steps of a good man are ordered by the Lord: and He delighted in His way" (Ps. 37:23). We want God's very best, and in return, He wants our very best. We owe God more than the 1 percent we give Him—ninety-nine and a half won't do, but ninety-nine more on our behalf is due. Push until you get to 100 percent. We sometimes ask one another, "Can you feel me?" Until you ask God and He says yes, you might want to keep on pushing until you give Him something He can feel!

Issues, Stop Hiding behind Trees

When I moved back to Ohio from Michigan, I saw old classmates that I hadn't seen in years. The people that I came in contact with almost brought me to tears. There are too many young people with their lives taken away because they thought drugs were the cool thing to do. People aren't taking these issues on drugs serious enough. Drug use is becoming more and more prevalent in our teens' and young adults' lives. What happened to the kids I went to school with can happen to anyone, smoking marijuana and drinking with everybody, and someone laced it!

These young people now are lost mentally, walking around not knowing if they are coming or going. I'm not just talking about the bad kids who people labeled and wished bad on them, saying they weren't going to be anything when they grew up, but I'm talking about straight-A students. Seeing this made me sad because every young person thinks it can't or won't happen to them, when everyone who indulges in these activities are candidates. Everyone thinks they're the precautious ones. It only takes one time, one wrong move with the wrong person you thought was right, and you too can be a victim.

A lot of the young adults started on marijuana. Once that high didn't last long enough or make them feel good anymore, they graduated to more powerful drugs. Doing any type of drugs not only shows that you have no respect for God, your life, or your loved ones, it also proves that you have no control over your mind or your actions, which makes you a weak individual. My favorite teacher, Mrs. Brown, used to always tell us that "a mind is a terrible thing to waste." So many young people just want to sit around and waste their lives away with drugs and ignorance.

The Bible tells us, "The carnal mind is enmity against God: for it is not subject to the law, neither indeed can be" (Rom. 8:7). Your mind must be lined up with God. If it's not, you're walking around in opposition or hatred toward Him. Let's revisit Adam and Eve for example. With them, it wasn't marijuana or crack cocaine; it was a piece of fruit. God told them not to eat of the tree, but they insisted and put something in their system that God told them not to. Like them, we try to cover up and hide behind leaves or, in some cases, the trees people are smoking.

With a lot of people who do things such as drugs and alcoholic beverages, it's not because they enjoy doing it or it tastes so great, many people use these things to cover the fact that they have issues. I've heard people when they were stressed, depressed, or tired say, "I need a drink" or "I need to smoke" because they felt like it calmed them down or took the pressure off them. They would always say, "I'll deal with that later," and of course, later never came. Instead of facing the music, people just rather blow it off!

Adam did something else people often do: point the finger. Adam pointed to Eve, and she pointed to the serpent. It seems so much easier to point the blame or focus off ourselves. We'll point to our parents not being there, or family members abusing us, and even the church being the reason why we have these issues in our lives.

The Bible says, "Casting all your care upon Him; for He careth for you" (1 Pet. 5:7). Instead of pointing the finger at man, give the problem to God! He cares for you so much He'll show you how to confront issues of your past and help you move on with a clean slate. It's not good to ignore things or try to cover them when God advises us that He's our present help in trouble (Ps. 46:1). You can do it God's way and get on course toward confronting your problems and getting forgiveness for your sins, or you can keep hiding behind trees and watch God leave you here with your issues! God isn't interested in playing hide-and-seek with you. He wants to be your covering so you're not running around naked and out of His will!

When Your Back Hurts and Your Knees Don't

There's a game we used to play at birthday parties and school functions called limbo. This game was played with a bar held up by a stand or two individuals. The objective of the game was to see who could stand up and bend backwards to the lowest level without knocking the bar over or touching it. The individual who was the most flexible won the prize. While the game was being played, bystanders would chant, "How low can you go?" If you ever played, you would know that you have to be pretty flexible to make it under the bar once it was lowered closer to the ground, which meant your back would be hurting.

In the world today, it seems like our young people have more backaches and pains than the older generation. Young folks today are always complaining of being tired, their feet hurt, along with many other problems. If young folks knew how to take the strain off their backs and use their knees more, they wouldn't always be sore. Youth today aren't as youthful or useful as they should be!

It seems like the older saints didn't always have to jump in the prayer lines because they got on their knees at home. Young people today don't want to have to go through anything. They don't want to bend over backwards, or endure until the end. They don't want to get low but want the prize.

Older saints were prayer warriors, which is why most of us are even who and where we are today. Somebody prayed for us, and I'm so glad they did! I've had jobs where I worked in a factory environment. In that line of work, you have to watch tapes in orientation on how to properly lift heavy objects. We were taught, when lifting heavy objects, to avoid using our backs and bend our knees.

Today the rule is still the same. When burdens are getting heavy and you're trying to lift heavy loads, in order for you to get the pressure off your back, you must use your knees: get down on them and pray. We should keep a prayer in our hearts and a praise on our lips at all times. There are going to be situations that only prayer and fasting will deliver us from. Christians are on their backs because they won't use their knees. You must come to the understanding that it's not your good grades, your good jobs, your good luck, and to some this might be a surprise, your good looks that can sustain you in this world, only your good prayers!

Prayer is so important that Jesus Himself prayed in every situation. He woke up early to pray, and when He had to bear his cross, He even prayed for His enemies. We are shown throughout the Bible that He prayed constantly and He was the savior who was given all power in His hands. How much more should we be praying being limited-power beings? You should be taking time out to pray just as you do for everything else important. Set a time daily for one-on-one time with God. Prayer should be more of a priority than going to school activities, social events, shopping, and anything else you enjoy doing.

Just like in the natural, if you don't communicate with others, how do you expect them to know what is going on in your life? How would someone know you lost a loved one, your job, you got married, or whatever else is going on? It's the same way with prayer in the spiritual. If you don't have conversation with God daily, how do you expect to hear what He has to say concerning His will for your life? There's no line of communication, praise, or worship. He wants to have a dialogue with you more than when it's about getting you out of trouble! You need to have an open line with God so you can get through and He can respond. God wants you in position to hear from Him because every day He has something to speak into your life. Every day He wants to pour fresh oil into your life; God wants to give you your daily bread daily.

Most of us know how it feels when certain people contact you when they're in need, and when they have money in their pockets, you're the last one they call. We dislike when people use us for their personal gain, but we turn right around and do it to God. He has the whole world on His mind. We're all on His daily to-do list, and here we are only going to Him when we're in emergency room situations. Now your scheduled appointments are interrupted before time because you stopped praying and messed up and need help right away! Your prayers shouldn't be the same after three and four years of being saved and delivered. You're still praying "Lord, I'm sorry," "Lord, I messed up again," and "Lord, I need help" every day!

At some point, you have to decide to live holy. Get over yourself so God can use you to be a blessing in someone else's life. How often do you go to God in prayer for others? Not often because you need Him to come to your problems all the time. You should be intercessors for widows, the fatherless, sick people, our men and women in prisons, and demon-possessed people, but here you are, still praying for just yourself. What's the difference between someone with an anointed life, a well-rounded life, and a life of favor over someone who lacks in these areas? The answer is simple: it's their prayer life, obedience, and relationship with God.

Young people, it's time to be where God's calling you to be—in Him. Scripture tells us that "the harvest truly is plenteous, but the laborers are few. Pray ye therefore the Lord of the harvest, that He will send forth laborers, into His harvest" (Matt. 9:37–38). Not only do you need to pray in the good but also in the bad. You need to pray not only when you're up but also when you're down.

Whether you're going through or coming out, God deserves to hear from you no matter what. You can't figure out why you can never get off your back, and a lot of times it's because you won't turn over and get on your knees. You don't have to be on your knees to pray, but prayer shouldn't be something you do only when you're backs against the wall! Next time you're in a position that isn't comfortable, go back to the basics: get on your knees and pray.

CHAPTER 6

Spring Break

Every year young people are excited to get vacation time from school. Grade school kids want to sleep in. High school students just want to hang out with friends. College students, most of the times they are looking for the best party spot to travel to for spring break. These few chapters will open your understanding of how the party life will cause you to be out of the will of God and be on a vacation spot where it's always hot and the Son refuses to shine!

May I Have This Dance?

Mardi Gras, J'ouvert, battle of the bands, All-Star Jams, block parties, all the way down to plain ole parties, everything revolves around music and dancing. I believe the church is ignoring who Satan is, the top producer in the world, having a master's degree in music.

The church is carrying on like some of the parties mentioned. The guys and girls have gone wild. Everybody's dancing like they're on Bourbon Street, being entertained at Mardi Gras. Our musicians are playing worldly beats like they're in the battle of the bands. We know better, but the young people have this thing where they're trying to hype up church to keep the feeling of the club atmosphere, and the older saints are putting up with this nonsense because some of them miss the club life. They use this time to reminisce on their good ole days.

Dance has become part of everything in God's house—praise dancers, step teams, drill teams, you name it. There are even gospel videos. Satan is working in his field of music since that's what he knows best. I was riding with an associate, and she had mentioned she had a good church song that I might like. The song she was referring to was "Jesus Walks." How confused is the world to think that a song that mentions Jesus but doesn't glorify or reverence Him is a church song? The way church has changed now, it might be appropriate, but the saints who know God for real know better than falling for this foolishness.

How have we become just as confused as the world? Why are we supporting R & B artists? Could it be because they give a shout out to God when they get their Soul Train Award for their worldly music? Or is it because some of the words they use—like *heaven*, *sky*, and *pray*—are in their lyrics? Any song that has a beat to dance to, the church will adopt it. God isn't impressed with us getting low unless it's down on our knees in prayer. He's not glorified when you're dropping it like it's hot unless it's your bad, sinful habits.

For some reason, I never got the impression that when David danced before God that it was a line dance, the monorail, or the Dougie. I can't visualize David dancing before the Lord like we try to imagine. David danced with all his might (2 Sam. 6:14). David was leaping and shouting. This wasn't a practiced step he prepared, so when the musicians played R. Kelly's beats, he had his cute two-step ready. (Sound familiar?) Church is more entertaining than these competition shows.

The only difference is we (the church) aren't voting the right ones off! Why do we make the comment "You can still dance, just change partners"? Anytime you change partners, you must have a change of heart first. You can't go into a new relationship without letting go of the old relationship. When we go before our king, we must be willing to let go of our past. We shouldn't want to be in the environment that reminds of our past. Think of a relationship you used to be in. When you two broke up, there were songs you wouldn't listen to, places you wouldn't go to for a while, and even people you didn't want to see because it reminded you of them. We can't bring God secondhand praises or rebound praises. If we don't praise Him, the rocks will praise Him.

In Psalm 100:4, it says, "To enter into His gates with thanksgiving and into His courts with praise." God gets the glory when we praise Him. God not only wants you to change partners, but He also wants you to change tracks. God wants to be reverenced, honored, and adored, not popped, locked, and dropped.

David was under the influence of the spirit, so you know it wasn't anything he picked up from the club or line dance classes. Can you give God an original praise, letting go of your rehearsed steps? We are playing clueless to how dances from the world is getting in our sanctuaries when we know some people are in the choir one day and on the dance floor the next. Our Sunday school teachers are teaching in church on Sunday mornings and become hip-hop dance instructors on Sunday nights.

Life will teach you it's not about your dancing, but it's in your praise and worship. A step you learned in the world won't bring you through. Only when you step out the world can you truly honor God and be delivered. When you take something from the world, don't bring it to the church. God's house is a place of reverence and glory. Do you expect God to be glorified in your dance that the world gave you? Church should never be viewed as a place where you feel like you kicked it. God is too holy of a god that He's not going to step off His throne to kick it with you. While Jesus walked the earth, the Bible never mentioned Him stopping over anyone's house to kick it.

This is why when the music is over, so many young folks are lost, text messaging, talking, or passing notes. It's another sign of spitting out the meat because all they can relate to is the beat. Young folks aren't being taught how to praise God. They don't understand that

God inhabits the praises of His people, not just people, but His people. We are told that when the praises go up, the blessings come down. But I must also add that when you praise and worship God, it must be of the right spirit and in truth. If your heart is still after the things of the world, then you're not in truth, and you have the wrong spirit. If you're still seeking to dance like and with the world, you didn't grab God's hand when you were switching partners. If God's Word would've said that we should look for God's ways to change in the last days, then I could see us thinking that maybe God is calling young people in a different way, but He said He does not change (Mal. 3:6).

When I got saved, I was young, and it didn't take all that. I wanted to get as far as possible from the things of Satan that caused me to go in circles. We have ushered Satan's spirit into the church through our new forms of what we call praise and worship. God is not sending us to any clubs, nor is He calling us to link up with the world to make new music. Money and lies have us so caught up that we're not hearing God's voice. God is asking for this dance, but don't say yes unless you're willing to let Him order your steps!

Can I Get a Light? Get Fired Up!

You will often hear this question when someone wants to smoke and doesn't have a lighter or matches. This same question is asked every day, but by God. The new generation of Christians wants to do and be like people of the world, and God is asking for a light. God has called us to be separate; we are in the world but not of the world. We are a chosen generation who God has called out of darkness to shine as lights.

The church has become more committed to pleasing young folks and converting the church to become like the world than being committed to converting the world to church. Not only are we confusing those we're trying to witness to, but in the process, some of our lights have dimmed. Trying to make everyone happy, there is no happy medium in God—either you love Him with your whole heart or you don't. Either you live a holy life or you'll spend eternity with Satan. God would rather have you be hot or cold (Rev. 3:15).

In my church, growing up, we used to sing a song that said, "This little light of mine, I'm going to let it shine." We need to go back to old-time religion even in this new day. God is seeking people, young folks, who will get fired up. He needs people that are not afraid to shine in darkness and who won't mind being set aside from the crowd. He wants to know whom He has on His side. When all odds are against you, will you still be faithful and fired up?

The Bible tells us, "In the midst of a crooked and perverse nation among whom ye shine as lights in the world" (Phil. 2:15). The Lord has let us know that not only does He need a light, but He also needs us to keep our fire burning when we do catch fire. God needs us to keep shining. How many situations have you been in when you have had the opportunity to be a light? How many times have you failed to witness? How many watts of light are you producing through your shine? Is it 25, 75, or 100 watts? Some people go off electricity, needing to be plugged in to things and people. Some are lanterns and run off oil, and have run out! We don't want to be like the new lights that are energy savers. We want to use as much energy as possible to help people get set free! You might be thinking your peers aren't trying to hear all that talk about Jesus. Regardless of what they want to hear, your job is to be about your Father's business. What we need to hear isn't going to always be what we want to hear.

I had this friend who was always a light for me way back in grade school. She would hear me saying bad things or doing things, and she would ask me what I was doing. She was shining her light. I would try to avoid her comments and act like it didn't bother me when it did. I wanted to be tough and play grown, but she knew my background, and she knew that wasn't me. No matter how much you ignore God, He will bring people your way to remind you of Him. Have you ever had to use the bathroom late at night, and you turned on the light, and your eyes could not focus because the light was too bright? That's how my friend was to me. Sometimes I would hate to see her coming when I was acting out because I knew she would come and make it hard for me to see or focus because her light was so bright.

Young people, we're called out of darkness into His marvelous light (1 Pet. 2:9). Can you go back in your mind when you first came into the light? When Jesus was center stage in all your acts? When you were all sold out? You were wearing your WWJD T-shirts and your WWJD bracelets. What happened to your fire that had you running to God? Was it a job, a prayer answered, a relationship, a car, or did you get burnt out? Whatever the case, you need to ask God to reveal it to you so you can request forgiveness. Allow God to restore your faith and rekindle your fire. We are told to cast off works of darkness and put on the armor of light (Rom. 13:12).

I can recall playing outside as a child. The thing I disliked most about the summer was all the bugs that came out. Thinking back, you would never see kids getting excited chasing hornets or bees, but you could bet once night came, they would be running around, chasing lightning bugs or fireflies. You might be saying, "Okay, so what's the point?" Thanks for asking. My point is, there are many things that are around us in the atmosphere, but not everything around us can disperse light. No matter what, you could always count on the few lightning bugs that came out to shine in darkness and became the light wherever they went.

We used to hit them out of the air onto the ground; sometimes we stepped on them and smeared their lights. As Christians, yes, sometimes your classmates or coworkers will try to run you down, catch you slipping, and spread rumors about you all around, but you need to still be a light. Get back to your passion for Christ, and if you have never been a light for Christ, catch fire. Our generation needs you. Our youth are dying because they are searching for something to follow and someone to be their light. They are reaching out for lights to grab. Turn on your light and lead them to Christ. God needs you to get fired up!

Sin and Lose on the Rocks

There was a popular song in the nineties that was called "Gin and Juice." To this day, this is a well-known combination at any bar. You will hear the bartender ask the customer how they want their drink, and a frequent reply would be, "On the rocks." In the vocabulary of someone who drinks, *on the rocks* means "with ice."

When I think about how they use rocks to replace ice, it's kind of strange to me. Ice is wet, slippery, and cold. Rocks are firm, solid, and mainly dry. They sound opposite but yet have the same qualities. One thing that I did discover about ice and rocks are they both slide easily, and when rocks are wet they too can be just as slippery. Another thing they both have is form, they can be very hard or solid, but if hit or dropped hard enough, both can crack under pressure, kind of like some of our salvation. Like the two, if they are wet and slippery, extra precautions must be taken.

Today our teenagers, as well as our young adults, hang out a lot. Some go to teen spots, and the older young adults go to clubs and bars. Simply because they want to be out around people their age and get away from home. When we put ourselves in those environments, we're on the rocks. We are setting ourselves up for all kind of things, mainly meeting the wrong people.

Some might say, "What's wrong with the club? I don't drink." Drinking isn't the only thing a child of God can do wrong in the club. If you're there to meet someone, what do the two of you have in common? If you're there to listen to the music, how is that magnifying God? If you go to shake what your momma gave you, how are you representing your Father and holiness? If you're going just to go, what does the Bible say about who we fellowship with? You have to be an example to your peers.

There are alternatives other than clubs and bars. Try bowling, skating, sports, or getting together with other saved and delivered people. I said "delivered people" because a lot of people are yelling that they're saved but are still living any way they please. Sin and lose is another way of saying it. The lose part is you'll miss out on heaven for a lifetime membership to a gym called hell, where you and Satan have eternity to work it out! People are still sinning and losing out on the blessings God has for them. It's a mixture just like the drink, except you won't get a high, as in high and lifted up with Jesus, by sinning. It's the fast life, disobedience, clubbing, and answering to fleshly commands.

Has your parent's ever told you not to go somewhere or not to do something, and you went anyway, or did what they said not to and you got into some mess? Out of all the people there, the trouble came right to you! Maybe you've heard, "Don't have sex," and you did and ended up with a lifetime bill—a baby or an STD. No matter how many witnesses we've seen before us, we have a mind-set that "It won't happen to me" or "I'm smarter than they were." Yeah right! God is saying He came that we might have life, and that more abundantly (John 10:10).

Nothing with life can stand the smell of dead things around them. The smell alone would run you from around them. Sin has a strong odor—worse than dirty wet clothes, worse than bad breath or even bad hygiene. Sin smells terrible, especially to God. The scripture sums it all up when it says, "Love not the world, neither the things that are in the world. If you love the world the father is not in him" (1 John 2:15). What would make people drink something that is called a spirit? Before you think about sipping an alcoholic drink, instead of getting a Budweiser, you need to be wiser. There's only one Spirit the Bible advertises, and that's the Holy Spirit. Either you'll be drunk in the Spirit or drunk by a spirit. Proverbs 20:1 says, "Wine is a mocker, strong drink is raging: whosoever is deceived is not wise." It's time to sober up and live with a purpose. I'm sure nobody likes to lose, and we all know God doesn't like sin. So keep in mind, if you don't get yourself together spiritually, your relationship with God will be on the rocks!

CHAPTER 7

Principal's Office

At one point or another, you might have ended up willingly or unwillingly in the principal's office, whether it was for help or discipline. In this world, God is the dean, and He has the principles that we must follow to make it to heaven. Don't settle for trouble or being in uncontrolled situations when God is in control and trying to prepare you in life so you can be blessed.

God Doesn't Need Your *But.* He Says It Stinks

Having four younger and three older nieces and nephews, when questioned, you'll hear the same excuses. The little ones, when told to do something, will blurt out, "But why doesn't so-and-so have to go to bed or eat all their food?" And you'll hear a response like, "Because I told you to." The older kids are the same, just a little different in their approach. You ask one of the older kids why they didn't do something like a chore, and they'll respond, "I was about to, but what had happened was . . ." or "I was about to, but . . ."

In both scenarios, whether they are worrying about why someone else didn't do something and the famous *but* excuse, we say *but* right before or after an act of disobedience. If flipped to God's point of view, God doesn't want us questioning His commands or making excuses for disobeying Him. Something else we do when God commands something after we told Him we will do whatever His will is and that we will go wherever He sends us, we add a but or set conditions. The first test or command that comes our way, we find ourselves saying, "Lord, I will do it. I will go, but I need another sign." If the Lord is already ordering your steps, why do you need so many signs and wonders before you obey? Could it be you really don't trust Him like you say?

So many young people can't trust God because they don't trust themselves. Our desires are still tangled up in the world. We are oblivious to the fact that just having God is enough. The promises of God should be enough. But why aren't they? When I asked young men and women why they don't attend church, their answers varied, saying that Christians were phony or that the pastors were pimping the people. No, it's not our fault why people say they are saved, but they don't live holy. Now the world expects an answer, and we point straight to the devil instead of disobedience!

Their response is, "Saved people are still going out, smoking, and drinking, so why would I go to church?" More questions, and the only thing we can say is, "Being saved isn't living that kind of life, but I don't know why they're doing it." The world is seeking answers, and we don't always know how to explain even when we know why! The church today is in such bad shape, but can we make it right for the next generation so they can avoid being humiliated like so many of us when we're asked these questions?

If we allow this behavior to take place in our generation, we'll let this nonsense continue for generations after us. If we stand up for holiness, this behavior can cease! If we we're honest when we made vows to God, there would be so many more saved and delivered people standing out, and not so many pretenders. More young people will be in church than clubs, and more young people will be prison guards than prisoners. God isn't a duplicate—He's an original. So why do we want to put the world's system in our church? God is always the leader being followed. Why aren't we following God's leading? When God speaks to you, don't be so quick to respond because you don't want to have to go back with a *but*. Seek God with a pure heart, and He will wash you from all the filth of the flesh and replace your *but* for His will! Remember God doesn't need your *but*. He says it stinks!

I've Fallen and I Can Get Up. I'd Like to Use a Lifeline

There's a popular game called *Who Wants to be a Millionaire?* This show gives contestants three options for help when they don't know the answer. They must tell the host they would like to use a lifeline. The three options are fifty-fifty, ask the audience, or they can phone a friend.

A story in the Bible that I will compare to this game show was when Jesus and the disciples were on the boat. It was like they said, "We would like to use a lifeline." Jesus was asleep in the boat, and the disciples ran into a problem: a storm was headed their way. They had three options: They could have used their fifty-fifty option by choosing to eliminate all their choices down to the top two, which were to fight the storm alone and possibly die or to go get Jesus and live. Secondly, they could have depended on others close by, which would have been like audience help. The third thing they could have done was to phone a friend or call on Jesus. They had to be sure that whichever option they used, it was their final answer. Without a doubt they chose to phone a friend, smart choice, because if you call on Jesus, He will answer prayers!

Our options are no different from the disciples' options. You don't always know the right answers, but where you get your help from is what makes the difference. There will be obstacles in life that you will have to trust God to be your lifeline decision maker in order to successfully overcome it. It might be for a major move in your life, relationships, school choice, career path, or just everyday personal attacks. When you're a young adult, there are so many options that you can take, but some will have you marching for 40 years if you don't make a wise final answer.

God is concerned about you and the decisions you make. He wants what's best for you. Your Heavenly Father is ready and willing to bless you, but because of your wrong choices and you wanting to be independent or choose to get help from everyone else, you put a limit on your blessings from God. Because of disobedience, you neglect God's will for your life.

As a young child, has your parents ever planned a vacation or special event, and every time you did something wrong, they threatened to cancel it? In the end, you still ended up going because your parents were excited about it more than you were. They wanted it for you because they knew you didn't have enough sense to know what they had in store for you. God is like that. He loves us so much and has such a mandate on our lives that He'll allow us to go through long storms and He'll even take things from us if they're blocking us from getting what He has for us. He'll allow so much to happen until you get to the point that you're ready to use a lifeline.

"I know the thoughts I have toward you, saith the Lord, thoughts of peace, and not of evil, to give you an expected end" (Jer. 29:11). Because God knows your beginning to your ending, He's steering you in the route of your blessings. With each passing year, you can look back a year or two and say, "If I only had done this or that, I would've been there by now." Whenever you step away from the thoughts and will of God, you send yourself on not only emotional detours but also spiritual detours. Each Christian is a lifeline to someone else. You are a disciple. Your first job or employer is God.

Have you ever been swimming and almost drowned? The lifeguard had to throw out a lifeline to help pull you out. A lot of young people are spiritually sinking and on their way down. Clearly you can see you're not living up to God's standards, still partying, being mean, treating your parents wrong, getting deeper in sin, still fighting, cursing, and everything else under the sun but not of the Son. Now your head is going under, and instead of kicking back to the top, you continue to add on more sins. Until you cry out to God and seek His face and turn away from sin, only then will you start to float back to the top. God will accept you with open arms because He is your personal lifeline.

You will learn that just having Jesus on board, at your reach, He is what makes the difference in your final answer. Today if you're on a boat that's rocking, the winds are raging, if water is seeping in, before you go under, try your faith and ask for a lifeline and believe your help is just one prayer away. It does matter which lifeline you choose, because only Jesus can save you!

Captain, Save Me. I want to be Saved!

A familiar passage in Daniel, we read about three men who needed God and didn't just need Him, but if God didn't step in, it would have been over for them. How many situations like this have we gotten into, whether it be on our own or someone else's mess?

In this story, these three men were told to bow down to a graven image. Whenever the people heard the sound of the flute, harp, cornet, and other music, they were to fall down to worship this image of King Nebuchadnezzar put before them (Dan. 3:5). If they didn't, they had to go into a fiery furnace. Have you ever been in a situation where someone tried to give you an ultimatum, whether it was blackmailing you because of something you did, said or for any kind of relationship purposes? If you have ever been in a predicament like this, you would either go along with their request or suffer the consequences.

In this passage, these three didn't bow down. They stood for something: they stood for God. Even though God wasn't visible at first in their situation, they still weren't going to bow. The king first asked, "Is it true?" He wanted to know if what he heard was correct. You know when some mess is about to get started, the person will come at you the same way. It's almost like the introduction when you're about to be put on the spot or called out.

The king asked, like people do today, hoping your answer will be the right one, No! They played it so cool and said, "We are not careful to answer thee in this matter" (Dan. 3:16). They exemplified the Matthew 10:19 faith. It says, "But when they deliver you up take no thought how or what ye shall speak: for it shall be given you in that same hour what ye shall speak."

How many people wait for God to respond? Not many people, or we wouldn't have folks getting cursed out so much! They were even questioned by the king, asking, "Who is this God that shall deliver you out of my hands?" Without hesitation, Shadrach, Meshach, and Abednego let the king know their god was able and that was enough said.

When we get into dilemmas and say God is able, we don't really believe it. We say it because it sounds like the proper religious answer. Maybe we even heard it before, and we liked the way it sounded. We must be convinced in our spirit that God truly is able. If we would get this truth in our hearts when tests or trials are before us, we will be able to stand on God being the final authority for our problems.

They waited on the Lord and believed He could do all things to the point they weren't going to bow. God wants this behavior from all His children. Regardless of how we see things or how we feel, we must trust in Him that whatever choice He makes for us, we know He has our best interests in mind. Whatever we go through that God allows, we have to be determined not to bow. When your peers are drinking and getting high, you need to say, "I will not bow." When your jobs are forcing you to step out of God's will, you need to be able to look at your boss in the face and say, "I will not bow." When everyone's out here doing their own thing, you need to be able to look temptations in the face and say, "I will not bow." Even when the situations cause the heat to increase as it did for them, "stand still, and see the salvation of the Lord" (Exod. 14:13). When you're in compromising situations, know the Captain is waiting to save you.

Just like the men who threw them in the fire were killed, Romans 12:19 says in short Avenge not yourselves. Vengeance is mine I will repay. God will be your strength when you're weak, so you don't have to bow to anything. God's Word says He's able to keep us from falling (Jude 1:24). The king went, looked, and asked, "How many people did we throw into the fire?" He was positive it was three. They all agreed it was just three. To the king's surprise, there were four, and they were no longer in bondage. Life has some of us in bondage to the sin we either have done or sometimes the sins we can't seem to let go of.

One thing about God is, not only will He step in the fire with us, but we will not get consumed, and He will make it easy for us to bear. Nothing in life is unbearable unless you refuse to go to the Captain for help. When you play sports, the referee or umpire will always ask for the captain when explaining the rules, if someone gets hurt, or for the coin toss. Well, likewise, we are on God's team, and He's our captain. So if you find yourself in a toss-up, hurt, or just needing to refresh on the rules of life, go to Him. Don't try to figure it out on your own. The Bible says, "Trust in the Lord with all thine heart; and lean not unto thine own understanding. In all thy ways acknowledge him, and he shall direct thy paths" (Prov. 3:5–6).

I have discovered people will try to destroy you or use your past against you, but the Lord will remember your sins no more. God will still step in the fiery furnace for you today. Your hair will still be in place, and you won't even smell like the mess you just came out of. One touch from God, you can be like Joseph in the pit one day, a hole full of your dirt, to sitting in high places. He's able to do "exceeding abundantly above all that we ask or think, according to the power that worketh in us" (Eph. 3:20).

Peter asked God to bid him to walk on the waters. When Peter saw he was moving in the impossible realm, he took his eyes off God and began to sink. It's like Peter cried out, "Captain, save me, I want to be saved." Whether you're like the three Hebrew boys, Joseph, or Peter, when God allows you to do the impossible as long as you stay focused on Him and not bow, or not think it's your own power, He will step in your fires, pits, and boats; point you towards the right direction; and save you if you want to be saved.

Shut Up, Listen from Your Gut!

Has there ever been a time when your parents sent you someplace, like to school or a family member's house, and you went somewhere else?

This is what happened to Jonah. He was told to go to Nineveh, and he went where he wanted to go! Sometimes God is trying to lead us one way, and we want to go the other way. Once we mess up, we find ourselves preaching the "if I had only listened" sermon. His disobedience caused him to be shut up in the gut of the fish! He was trying to escape the Lord's purpose for him and almost got eaten alive.

Jonah 1:3 tells us he paid the fare to get away. How often do we end up paying for our disobedience one way or another? Jonah paid double for his trouble in trying to escape from God. When you run from God, you will always end up getting caught. You'll find out getting caught up isn't always bad, at least not in Jonah's case. Jonah was the cause of fear and destruction to come upon everyone around him. He noticed that he had to be a man and take responsibility for his actions, so he requested they throw him overboard. The Lord had big plans awaiting Jonah and a big fish on assignment waiting to shut him up!

The Lord has our lives already planned out, and God sends people our way who are assigned to be there. When God tells us to do something or go somewhere, it's important to listen. Once the mouth of the fish is shut, once we get in a dark area or a no-win situation, only then will we willingly sit and listen to God. Maybe your gut experience was a teen jail, an adult prison, a hospital, or maybe a bad situation; God has a way of shutting us up where we can't get out. All God wants from us is obedience so we can avoid all the detours that Satan will try to put in our way.

Most people will sacrifice freedom and many other things in life before they follow directions from God. If you're going to make a sacrifice, let it be your praise, as Jonah did. Jonah 2:9 says, "But I will sacrifice unto thee with the voice of thanksgiving." After he sent up his praises, God allowed the fish to vomit him onto dry land.

The key to coming out of anything is through your praise. Some people learn from the first lesson, while others just don't learn except destruction takes place. The story concludes with Jonah doing what the Lord told him to do in the first place, which was going to Nineveh. So learn from Jonah that if you do things God's way, you won't have to pay your way out of trouble or hear God from your gutter situation.

CHAPTER 8

Hook Me Up

When a young person is interested in someone, they will ask their friends to see what's up with that person. They will say to their friend, "Hook me up." The next few chapters speak to the ladies and guys on a personal level of what they should expect or what they should look for in others. It also will speak to the desires that young saved adults face.

Are You in Popular Demand or a Popular Demon?

Young men, this question is to you. The world has taken so many of our young men either to prison or the grave. Young men have such a love for money, power, and respect that they will use any means necessary to get what they want. Wanting money, they are risking their freedom to sell drugs. Wanting power, they are carrying guns and killing one another. Thriving to be respected they don't care whom they have to step on to move higher.

We learn in 1 Timothy 6:10 that "the love of money is the root of all evil." We see this to be true just by reading the paper or watching the news with just how much evil it has caused. Money is a big reason why men won't bow to God, and sometimes it's the only reason they bow but it's the wrong reason. Money has become their master. We're told, "No man can serve two masters: for either he will hate the one, and love the other; or else he will hold to the one and despise the other. Ye cannot serve God and mammon" (Matt. 6:24).

So because God is all-seeing and all-knowing, He knew there would be this barrier between men and women that would cause them to grab hold of something other than the love of Christ. What's not popular nowadays is a young man that's sold out for Christ. You don't see many young men who are willing to bow down to something they have never seen or physically touched. In Romans 8:12, it says, "Therefore, brethren, we are debtors, not of the flesh, to live after the flesh." You hardly see or hear about men who get on their knees and get their direction from God. You are to "put ye on Christ, and make no provision for the flesh, to fulfill the lusts therefore" (Rom. 13:14).

Many people don't understand that there's a difference between the popular boy, a man, and The Man! Being the boy is what most guys set out to be when they're younger—the boy being the one with all the ladies, nice clothes, nice hair, nice jewelry, suave personality, nice cars, and pockets full of money. The boy wants to impress women with his charm and his smooth game, always competing for the top spot.

Then you have a man. He's someone who's secure with himself because he knows he's in the hands of God. He understands that he doesn't have to be flashy because his fruit will tell his story for him. He doesn't have a need for a lot of women; he's satisfied with one. A man is caring, loving, gentle, and not selfish.

While the boy is being young-minded, caught up in the outward things, he is unaware those are the adolescent stages you go through before becoming a man. A man is a hard worker to provide for himself, and if he has a family, he will provide for them as well. A man doesn't look for handouts, while the boy won't mind a woman supporting them or living with his mom until he's forty. Only a boy looks for a woman for what he can get from her, while a man seeks a woman for what he can give to her. The boy blames another man for his shortcomings; a man rolls with the punches despite his obstacles and moves forward.

The boy has the law set a price on how much his kids are worth, and when he should see them; a man supersedes and isn't limited to a dollar amount or visitation limits. While the boy will find a reason why he laid his hands on a woman, a man would never find it appropriate to abuse a woman no matter what. The boy will treat a woman how she acts, while a man will treat a woman like a lady regardless of how she acts because he has more respect for himself to ever put a woman down.

I can go on and on comparing the differences. The bottom line is, a real man lines his life up with God's Word. Being popular won't always be in demand, but being in Christ will protect you from being a popular demon. The only way you can make demons flee and live an abundant life is by knowing and following after The Man, who is Christ Jesus!

Girlfriend, Your Makeup Doesn't Match!

This is to all my ladies, my sisters in Christ. I grew up in a household with two saved, sanctified parents. I never had to experience or see a lot of things that many young women go through now. There is an old song, "I'm Coming Up on the Rough Side of the Mountain," for myself that was never my testimony. I didn't have to go through anything growing up, fighting parents, drinking, doing drugs, or witness the street life. Any and everything that I experienced was once I became a young adult and I moved out of town.

It was once I was older and away from my parents that I tried to do more things to feel like an adult. I used to try the parties and the clubs, and for some reason, I went and didn't know why once I got there. I didn't drink, smoke, or dance. I would always get teased by my cousin for churching up a club outfit. I was trying to be something and someone that I was not, which was why my makeup didn't match. I was made up to be a woman of God from birth! I was raised totally opposite from the type of person I was trying to be. I wasn't following the characteristics that made me who I should have been in Christ.

I caused myself to go through things that I didn't have to because I was trying to be a cover girl. I was trying to cover the fact that God had His hand on me, and I didn't want to accept God's will for my life at that time. I wanted to be like everyone else. I wanted to be looked at and liked by all the guys. For some reason, I felt I needed attention—which, by the way, was the wrong attention. It was an insecurity that I needed God to fill, and not man.

Many insecure women are in the church. This is one of the reasons we get men who don't mean us any good, running game on us, saying things like, "I would go to church if I had a good church girl like you." Right then, we cover for him and say, "Maybe he will start going to church with me!" If he's not going for what God's done for him, it won't be long until he stops going for you.

When I was in school, there were certain teachers I would act up with, and with other teachers, I was an angel. Once teachers got together to talk about their bad students and my name came up, some would say, "No, not her," while others would say, "Yes, her." The ones who knew me said, "No, that doesn't sound like her character." Then I would get fussed at by the teacher who I actually liked! Sometimes we get around certain people and put up a front as if we're this bad person because we think it will get us acceptance from our peers. This behavior continued until I took a look at myself in the mirror and asked, "Who am I?" For some reason, my attitude didn't match how I felt on the inside. I knew I had greatness in me, but I couldn't see it because I was overly made up. I was wearing my makeup too thick, almost like a mask covering my real identity. Even though I knew I was fearfully and wonderfully made, I was trying to make myself over, only to look like a monster.

We say we're saved, yet we're so high-minded no one can say anything to us. We say we love God but hate one another. We claim to be disciples, and we're not even good examples. We are walking around in a world full of confused people with all these different shades on their faces. Women, we are called to a special place in God. The Bible speaks on women as virtuous, and the value of a virtuous woman (Prov. 31:10). We are also looked at as the glory of man (1 Cor. 11:7).

Women allow men to play them like they're only good to dance in their videos while they disrespect themselves half-naked. These men write all their raps and songs calling women everything but a child of God, and we continue to settle being disrespected. You should never settle. You're the head and not the tail, so you shouldn't be the tail in videos, on dance floors, or in sports. When you watch videos, those men have clothes, hats, boots, and hoodies on, while women only have on bikinis! The men are the ones that are promoting something, making all the money, and the women are the ones naked. Male athletes don't wear their shorts tight or short, but again, the ladies are half-naked. Why are you so foolish? You're getting a little bit of money to degrade yourself and you're entertaining their fans while they are making millions of dollars? Don't be so desperate! Women, we're greater than what we settle for. You're happy that men are calling you sexy, while God is disappointed because He made you to be called holy. The Bible says the women shall prophesy (Joel 2:28). God has spiritual need for you.

Ladies wanting to be strippers, gold diggers, video girls, and groupies, chasing after men, this is in total contradiction to God's Word! God has set you above all that. Why put yourselves in degrading positions in life and then cry about that nobody wants or respects you? A man pleaser will always end up dissatisfied.

I discovered while watching the reality show *America's Next Top Model* that many of the women have so many issues and will expose themselves in front of the world, hiding behind made-up faces, covering their flaws on the outside, and a total wreck in the inside. The modeling world moves so fast they don't have time to confront their situations, so they change costumes and jump on the runway. Like so many women, they change their appearance and run away from their problems!

Ladies have even lowered their standards on how they communicate with one another. Why would you be so ignorant to call each other disrespectful names? You limit your own destiny when you don't see yourself how God sees you. Some women feel unworthy to be used of God because they have done and been through so much. You are the very one God needs. He can use your testimony to reach other young ladies. He can use your transformation to transform some of the people you used to do your dirt with.

Many women have had their faces beat up so bad by Satan that makeup won't even cover the scars. Some ladies need God to just do a complete makeover, starting with a facial. God wants to clean your pores and pour His love into you. He wants to reapply all the things that you were stripped of. God will start by applying your foundation. He specializes in building confidence while He hides you in His shadow. When your foundation is properly applied, He'll drop in your spirit all the things you need to transform into that person He said you were from the beginning. He'll apply your eye shadow so you can look bolder for Him. He will apply your eyeliner thicker so He can highlight things you see and how you see yourself. God wants to pluck your eyebrows so you don't look surprised when He performs miracles throughout your life. He'll even put a little blush on your cheeks so you can smile again. Some ladies can't afford Mary Kay, MAC, Fashion Fair, or Clinique. Some can only afford Wet n Wild, and you're acting just like that! For some people, the name makes a difference. Whether it's affordable or not, if you need coverage, you'll buy it at any cost. Know that you are covered by the blood!

Storms and strongholds are something we all have to go through, but if you're made up by the hands of the potter, He can take a plain ole mold and make a beautiful piece of art. Yes, you might pick up a few scratches along the way, but God has you covered. If you're not living by the standards God has set for you, you're living beneath your birthright. You are somebody in Christ, so get in God's chair and allow Him to make you over because, girlfriend, your makeup doesn't match!

I Desire to Be Desired!

We have a lot of young adults who grew up in life without their fathers present. A lot of young ladies were never loved by a man and were always taken advantage of. A lot of young men have never seen an example of a real man. Most young men and women are looking for that perfect mate who won't cause them any more pain or hurts. Young people are getting to the point where they are tired of dating because of all the games people play.

Many women desire to be a wife, mother, and successful career woman. Most women are saying, "I desire to be desired!" Over and over, God hears this request from men and women who are searching for love and no more lies. It's not satisfying single women to hear, "For God so loved the world he gave his son." Now they want some of these earthly women to give up their sons. So many mothers aren't making their sons grow up and be men, wanting to shelter them forever. So many men desire to be husbands, but they feel like they don't have much to choose from. Either the women have low self-esteem, no confidence, or they have been abused so much they can't accept being loved when a real man shows up!

What we must realize is that our first love should be Jesus. We should love Him so much that we start to take on His characteristics until He sends us our mate. Most people are looking for the perfect mate. If that's the case, you should consider staying in a relationship with God forever. No one is perfect but Him. On the physical side, Jesus isn't what we expected because with the natural eye, you can't see or touch Him even though you can see His works, and feel His presence, women tend to want a little bit more of a visual and someone we can physically touch.

One thing we must show God is faithfulness; we must surrender our all to Him. Women want a husband but can't submit their will to God. Men want a good wife and can't be trusted with his finances taking care of the things of God in His house. How will you run your household when you don't support God's? You want a mate, but you are constantly cheating on God in your prayer lives, and you won't even read His Word, which are personal love letters from God.

When it comes to our relationship with God, people ask if it's in vain, praying and fasting, and nothing is changing. The same people can be in an abusive relationship that's not going anywhere, and they never once question if it's in vain. When you get to the desperate stage, you'll find yourself compromising and settling for anything that comes your way. Instead, why not accept the Word of God? It says, "The Lord wants you to trust in Him at all times; ye people, pour out your heart before Him: God is a refuge for us" (Ps. 62:8). We allow Satan to manage our self-esteem and who we are in Christ. We're made in His image, so we should feel good just knowing that we don't have to settle for anything less than the full promises of God.

So often women will allow men to run over them and talk to them any kind of way, and because he still takes them out from time to time, they feel loved, or so they say. Ladies, when you're disrespecting yourselves by degrading your bodies in the way you dress, act, or getting high and drunk, a man will view you as trash. Let's face the fact most guys' only chore is to take the trash out. You might get a few dates out to dinner or to a movie, and he might even handle you with care, but when he's tired of carrying you around (once he thinks you're trash), like all trash, eventually you'll be kicked to the curb!

We are assured through God's promises that "the desires of the righteous shall be granted" (Prov. 10:24).

I can't count how many times I've heard women say a man was too nice and that something had to be wrong with him! Why do women assume that a man can't treat them right without something being wrong? This comes from putting a price on something that's priceless. Most women don't know their worth, and they have the bar set so low they don't feel like they match up to the competition! For some reason, our minds can't comprehend that we should expect excellence and the best in every area of our lives. Some people still can't imagine how much God loves them and that He died while we were sinners.

When you prove that you are ready, God will allow a spiritual transformation. He'll fade out as your mate and replace himself with a physical being. Every time you allow someone in your life that shouldn't be there, you prolong the process.

Sooner than later, you'll figure out God doesn't need your help. When we try to help, we pick out people and make excuses for them or get with people for all the wrong reasons, wanting to have sex, and you end up with just that—a sexual relationship. Nothing spiritual will come out of it. You like them because of money. When the money's gone, your relationship will be gone. If you like them because they look good, when something happens and they don't look the same, guess what, neither will your relationship. Whatever your motive, you will reap it in the end. More than likely if it's any motive other than true love and divine connection, it's already at the end.

The law of reaping and sowing applies to your entire life. Wait on the Lord and don't settle. The Lord will give you whatsoever your heart desires when you're faithful to Him and put Him first. Your heart can't be bought in four lifetimes, and your mind should never be sold out to anyone. Your heart, mind, and soul belong to God. When God thinks you're ready, He'll send you a tenant to take up residency. Until God fills the house, don't allow anyone to rent, lease, or buy because you're God's property! You were bought with a price, so put your Sold sign up.

Let Me See Your Gift. What's on the Inside?

One day I asked the Lord what my purpose was in life. I knew He had something for me, I just couldn't identify what it was. Most of the time, you ask the question, not knowing the answer lies within you. Everyone is equipped with what they need to succeed in life. Your gift is usually something you have always been good at or something that your talents point towards.

Since I was a young girl, anytime I was upset, I would go write. In school, we would get writing assignments, and the teacher would always be impressed. Knowing I was very good at writing, I still asked God to reveal my gift. Writing was something that I loved to do and something I was passionate about. Your gift isn't a choice—it's already in you. It's not like a gift registry. You don't check off things you want to be gifted in. God chose your gift before you were born.

Every chance I got, I exempted the thought of writing being my gift. Like myself, I'm sure you can find several things you're good at, but I found that they usually all tie together to create the perfect gift. What is a gift? It's something bestowed voluntarily without compensation, a present. Jesus didn't wait until your birthday or Christmas to give you a gift. You have received many gifts from God before you were even physically created or formed in your mother's womb. He didn't just give you what's inside of you, but He gave you what was inside of Him—Jesus. Because of Jesus, we don't have to endure a lot of things—like sickness, poverty, or hell—because Jesus was the gift given as our one-for-all sacrifice. He let us know that eternal life is also a gift to His children (Rom. 6:23). There are also spiritual gifts; you know them as the gift of the spirits: word of wisdom, knowledge, gifts of healing, miracles, prophecy, divers kinds of tongues, and interpretation of tongues (1 Cor. 12:8–10).

On special days, when people give you a gift, or present, how many people do you know who never opened it to see what was inside? Probably nobody! If there's no other reason besides anxiety, you're going to open the gift. How would you feel if you bought someone something for their birthday, and you go over their house, and it's still wrapped up a year later? You would be fussing about how you could have saved your money if you knew they were going to let it sit.

How do you think God feels? This is how God wants us to feel about the undeserved gifts He's given us. We should be excited to express our thankfulness for His blessings. With all the gifts He has given out, people are content year after year just letting their gift sit in an inactive status. Sometimes people confuse their gifts and talents. Your gift is your purpose; even though you have talents, it just means you're good at something, but the gift is what makes room for you. Take someone who can sing, which there are many people who can, then there's someone who just has an anointing in their singing. One of them is talented, but the one with the anointing is gifted.

We seem to always want someone else's gift. When you hear someone who can sing, the first thing you'll say is, "I wish I could sing." You have your own gifts you're not using. You look at other people's careers—like athletes, musical artists, and television stars—and want their lifestyles. God has put greatness in you too, but you won't know unless you look within yourself and not everybody else. Your gift is in you, and the world is waiting for your gift to be revealed. You need to throw yourself a coming-out party and manifest your gift because we're all waiting to see what's on the inside of you.

CHAPTER 9

Most Athletic

We have all heard the title Most Athletic especially when it comes to sports and superlatives in school. This is the person who played the most sports, excelled the highest in the sports they played, or is pretty good at playing the game! There are athletes in the Bible that we overlook all the time, Jesus being one. Read and find out why Jesus is the MVP of all.

Fighting Satan, Take a Knee if You Bout It

We're in a day where Satan is coming at us before the bell rings. He's not giving us the chance to put our gear on. So many times we fight without the proper protection. We get in a bout with Satan, and we don't have our headgear on, which is the helmet of salvation, leaving our head open to get banged up and Satan the opportunity to drop negative thoughts in our minds. We don't have our mouthpiece in, and that's how we allow anything to come out without thinking. We're not in our proper stance, not having our feet shod in preparation. We're not strong in the Word, so we don't know what God has said about our situation. Many of us don't have anything in our hands like the shield of faith. We need the shield to block out things the enemy throws at us.

I'm sure like myself, Satan has won a few rounds with you. Often we just stand in the ring and allow Satan to come at us with the same punches, the same situations, the same temptations, and the same lies, jab after jab of all the combinations we've seen before. Some of them are so familiar that we move in the path when we see it coming, setting ourselves up to get knocked out because we are so used to losing. How many times have you seen the same traps and allowed yourself to fall for it? By now both of your eyes are black and swollen, yet you continue with the fight, knowing that if you take a knee your strength can be renewed.

The scripture tells us to "call upon me in the day of trouble; I will deliver thee and thou shall glorify me" (Ps. 50:15). You can take a knee and continue to fight, throw in the towel and quit or stand there and keep playing with Satan until he knocks you out! David and Goliath were in a bout, and in this story, we find that it doesn't matter how big your opponent or how giant it is, God is able to bring you out even if He chooses by way of a TKO! Everyone was opposed to David fighting this battle because of his size and age, but when people count you out, God will help you remember things He's already brought you through.

David went back and mentioned to the doubters at ringside how he defeated a lion and a bear. He was confident that he could defeat Goliath in the same manner as he did the wild animals. Life has a way of throwing situations so quick, and we're good at yelling what we can't do instead of quoting the scripture that tells us that we can do all things through Christ who strengthens us. Let the Lord fight for you!

Even with David being young, he never doubted the outcome being in his favor. David knew he was small and young, but he had giant faith and courage. David asked some critical questions. First, he asked, "What shall be done to the man that kill this Philistine, and take away the reproach from Israel? For who is this uncircumcised Philistine?" (1 Sam. 17:26). David wanted to know what the consequences were.

When we allow Satan to put us in the ring to fight, we need to act out our authority. Don't just jump in the ring, but ask some questions. Just as professional boxers watch tapes of their opponents, you need to review what combinations Satan has already thrown at you! David, in a few verses later, asked, "What have I now done?" Then he asked, "Is it not a cause?" He knew he had a purpose and a reason for being there. Behind every trial or test, there is a cause. Behind every giant test, there is a giant victory.

David's brother knew Goliath had been fighting from his youth, so it was like a professional boxer fighting an amateur. David had no fear with God on his side. We are trying to fight with our bad attitudes, guns, and disobedience, when all we need is the stone that the builders rejected, who is the Chief Cornerstone—Jesus! If you would grab a hold of Jesus, He is the only rock that you'll need in life's battles.

One time I put myself in a fight that I shouldn't have been in. I went out of town with a couple of friends. One of them was my best friend at one point. We started talking about things in the past, and the conversation converted to a shouting match. Both of us flew off the handle over things that were done and over with. It ended with words that weren't pleasant, and it should have never gone that far. Even in my state of anger, I cried out to God in my spirit to keep me, but in my heart I was ready to fight. I knew before I would have reacted out of anger and never considered God until the damage was done. He would've sent ministering angels to my corner but I wouldn't take a knee. I could've showed God's keeping power. Instead, I allowed Satan to knock me down. Don't throw in the towel and give up on God, take a knee and give it to God! It took me a few weeks to give it over to God and not allow that old man to resurface to the fighter I used to be BC (before Christ)! I had to acknowledge that God had changed me a lot from the old man (but I still had a ways to go), while Satan wanted to keep beating the old thoughts in my head. David's only strategy or skill was his faith in God. In most bouts, all you will have is your faith. That's why knowing Him as well as His Word is so critical.

Notice before Saul sent him out, he protected David's head. It's critical not to let the enemy get in your head! When you read the story, it tells us that the stone sunk in Goliath's head (1 Sam. 17:49). David finished him off by taking Goliath's weapon and cutting his head off. When Satan wants to challenge you, God will take his weapon and defeat him with it. Bouts sometimes start off with Satan trying to destroy your dreams, make you doubt God, and even take your focus off God. Like David you might get a KO or your fight might go the distance, all twelve rounds. You may fall a few times but get back up. You might get bruised throughout the entire fight, but if you can hold on until the bell, God, your judge, will ensure the score cards rule in your favor. God is telling you not to worry and have no doubt. Step in the ring with your enemies, your issues, and your fears, put your hands up, and let's get ready to rumble!

How Much You Want to Bet, All or Nothing?

Life for many is like a game of chances. People take chances with everything. Men will bet or gamble on just about anything—cars, games, races, and sports, you name it. Christians take chances every day in the decisions we make and the things we do. One of the chances with the highest risk is when we sin against God, not knowing if we'll get the chance to make it right.

Every great person in the Bible took chances, but theirs was of obedience, faith, and trust. One person that I think about when it comes to someone who took a huge chance is Elijah. He asked a prophet in Mount Carmel, "How long halt ye between two options?" (1 Kings 18:21). They were double-minded people, and the Bible says, "A double minded man is unstable in all of his ways" (James 1:8). It was like Elijah said, "How much you want to bet your God doesn't deliver, all or nothing?" They were up for the challenge, Elijah against Baal's four hundred fifty men. Sometimes at school, in the workplace, and in different activities you attend, it's you against the crowd. People are always watching to see what you're doing or how you'll respond to various situations.

These men called on their God and jumped around the altar, and still there was no answer. The man of God said, "Maybe your God is asleep. Many times, the devil tries to play our minds like Elijah played with their minds, wanting us to believe God isn't coming through. He wants us to see others being blessed and think God is sleeping on us. Rebuke that thought and cast it down as soon as the devil comes at you with it. Our God never sleeps or slumbers. When you're obedient and faithful and don't get weary in well doing, you will be blessed.

Satan will try to make you compare how you live with others. You can't envy lifestyles of the rich and godless. They're not only selling drugs, movies, and their bodies, but they are selling their souls. God promises blessings, abundance, prosperity, and overflow. Satan is the enemy who wants to steal, kill, and destroy you. Satan is full of deceit.

By the evening, it was Elijah's turn to prove his god, his turn to put it all on the table. He had his stones, built an altar, and poured water on the sacrifices and wood (1 Kings 18:33). He had the formula of receiving from God. He prepared a sacrifice and then reverenced God. Elijah knew that he had to humble himself to get a blessing. Lastly all he had to do was step back while God showed up and showed out. Next time you're in a gambling mood, don't go to the lottery line, casinos or pick up any dice. Go get the Word of God and bet all or nothing on what God says He would do. Follow Elijah's regimen, and watch God come through for you too. God can't fail. He will show up. How much do you want to bet? With God, it's your all or nothing!

MVP, He's Got Game!

We are living in a time where sports are becoming more popular by the year. With all the new talent, whether it's in baseball, football, basketball, boxing, or golf, each player feels they are the next best athlete to excel in the sport they're playing. If sports aren't on the TV, the guys are playing them on their video games. Sports are in high demand. I happen to love sports as well. Not as much as the guys, but I will play and watch them from time to time.

When I was in school, I played basically every sport. In middle school, I was the athlete of the year. My least favorite sport to play but one of my favorites to watch was basketball. I didn't care for all the running up and down the court that seemed to get longer the more I ran! I love to watch those who have mastered their sport and enjoy playing it.

One player who enjoyed the sport of basketball was Michael Jordan, the face behind the saying "I want to be like Mike." Michael is one of my favorites of all time. He took the sport to another level in his ability to carry and lead his team to great comeback victories. Another player I like is LeBron James, who is also known as King James. We all know he's not the one who wrote the Bible, but he's proven he can write his own plays on the court! He has shocked the world being a young player with such phenomenal court vision and skill level.

Both Michael and LeBron will go down in history for not only their abilities to score but also their abilities to glide through the air, which we call hang time. Both of them can slam dunk on just about anyone. Their ability to sell out crowds and draw people from all over is amazing. Every sport has what they call an MVP (most valuable player). This is the top-notch of the team. It's usually the team leader and role model. The MVP has the know-how on how to make things happen. My all-time favorite who I would pick as my MVP would have to be Jesus. He is also known as a king, the King of Kings, and many will testify that they want to be like Jesus. He gets the award not only because He draws the biggest crowds or because He's the most talked about, being the most loved and hated, but He has the best hang time. Talking about someone who can carry a team! He could have passed the ball, but he didn't. It made Him drive harder to the hole (grave)! He hung with nails in His hands and feet, through a crown of thorns and whips all over His body. He hung while He was constantly beaten and spat upon, while carrying the sins of the whole world, getting pierced in His side and being laughed at.

People came from all over to see His hang time that lasted for hours. Just when they thought they fouled Him out of the game for good, He got up with all power in His hands. He is my choice as the go-to man. When you have a problem, you can throw it to Him. When your bills are due, pass it to Jesus. When someone is on your back, give it to Him. Not only is He never going to be forgotten, but every generation will know Him. He'll forever be the king because He never lost His victory. Every coach wants Him on their team because they checked His stats and records, and they still haven't been beaten. He's dependable and has never had a broken bone. He can adjust to anyone and work with any group of people.

Today Jesus is saying to you and I that He would love to be on teams with us. So when it's your turn to pick, call on Him. He wants to make you a player, not a playa! Just remember, when life is pressing you, He'll break up the double-team action and take on your problems man-to-man, so you know when you travel with Him, He'll always have your back until you can get up from the flagrant fouls of the devil. He'll give you time to get your composure together so you can rebound to your feet. God doesn't want you out of bounds or on the sideline. He made you a starter from jump ball. So get out there, and play smart with the rest of the Saints. You can't go wrong when you're teamed up with the greatest MVP of all time—Jesus!

CHAPTER 10

Class Tripp . . . ing

Since grade school, I can recall taking class trips. Some were fun and exciting, while others were very boring. What you are about to read are stories about life and how Satan can have you not only on trips where you're running from him and your troubles, but he'll also have you tripping! When you call out to Jesus for help, He will save you so you don't have to back down to Satan or anyone else.

When Satan's Tailgating, Keep on Trucking

I had one of the most exciting experiences ever. I drove 18-wheelers for a short time. It was one of the most amazing challenges I had ever been faced with. Being a female, and I had never driven anything half its size before, enhanced the challenge. One major lesson I learned was just because something appears to be bigger than you, it doesn't mean you can't control it.

The 18-wheeler looked huge to me. I thought to myself, *There's no way in the world I'm going to be able to handle this big boy!* I saw something bigger than me and automatically ruled myself out. When Satan comes at us, we look at the situation and try to size up with it, already knowing we're physically smaller. Since we serve a big God, we shouldn't be worried about how big the problem is "because greater is he that is in you than he that is in the world" (1 John 4:4).

New drivers were really put to the test when it came time to back up. This was something that sometimes I could do, but there were many times I struggled. When Satan backs us up, we become disoriented. For some reason, the theory of backing a truck had me this way. They told us it was left to loosen and right to tighten, or lefty-Lucy righty-tighty. In a car, you turn the wheel the direction you want the back of the car to go. In a truck, you turn the wheel the opposite way.

You can think of it this way: when you're faced with conflicts that back you up in a tight spot, remember to loosen those things you left behind you, and as you press toward the mark, tighten your hold on what's right, and you'll end up in between the lines. Things that are behind you are your past. Let it go, and keep moving. There will be times in your life when you choose another highway, and people will try to hold you to your old routes. They don't seem to see your changes when they're positive, but as soon as something negative happens, they're hot on your trail. Satan is good for retracing your past.

Sometimes it's good to look back in your rearview mirror just to touch base and see where God has bought you from. You're just glancing while still in drive because you're moving forward towards the things that are ahead of you! There is nothing more annoying than talking to an extra saved older person who was never a sinner—those saved folks who act like everything you do is the worst thing they ever heard of when they were worse than you. They forgot they were once young and made mistakes too.

There was another term I learned from driving that relates to how you have to handle people like that. It was called *bump and run*. This term meant that instead of going through all the gears, you would hit a gear and skip a gear or two. This eliminated you from going through all the gears individually. You will come across folks that you'll bump into in and out of church, speak to them, and run. Say hello, and keep it moving. When you are a newly born-again saint, you need this. It will help you pace yourself around people until your faith is built up to tolerate them. Another test was learning every part of the truck as well as being able to name and identify them. It was helpful to be able to identify the parts because it helped me gain more confidence before the skills test. There were three parts involved in the skills test: the pretrip inspection, basic control, and on-road test. You identify what you're going through, calling things as you see them by it's name. You point out who's in control, and lastly, you sit back and go for the ride!

The actual skills test was when I had to put all the knowledge attained together. Sometimes on your test, you may take narrow roads or get in tight spaces. Other times, you might take the city streets. If you're lucky, you'll get the straightaway or highway and go full speed. When the enemy comes your way, don't back up, don't go around him, and don't move over; go head-on with him. If you allow him to have the wheel, he will drive you out of control. When Satan is on your bumper, take the straight path, and don't let him make you change the course God has you on. When it seems like you're in a standstill or a jam, wait on the Lord and be of good courage. And when you start moving again, don't look back, keep on trucking.

I See Smoke but No Fire in the House

There had been times when I had been up late watching a good show or waiting for one to come on, and I felt like I had the energy to stay up for a little while longer, so I decided to look for something to eat that wouldn't take long to prepare. Wrong move! Once I put the food on, my eyes began to get heavy, and before I knew it, I fell asleep. Hearing the alarm go off, seeing smoke, I panicked and looked around to see if there was a fire in the house. I would say, "Thank God, it was a false alarm."

This might have been something you have experienced up late making a snack. Now I'm finding it more and more in the house of God. You might be asking yourself in the church, how? In the house of God, it isn't the food we're cooking. It's the prepared food that we're feeding our souls. False alarms would be our pastors, deacons, evangelists, ushers, choir members, and youth. Everyone is clouding the house with smoke with all their jumping and shouting, but they're not living right. The smoke usually comes before the fire, but in the house of God, the smoke is coming after our fire. In other words, the fire of God isn't in the church. The anointing and spirit of God isn't present. God wants us to be like spiritual smoke detectors. Wherever we are and the air isn't clear, we should be able to sense it, and sound the alarm. We should not sit there like our batteries are dead, but we should be like Energizer batteries and keep going and going, praying and pressing, until deliverance takes place and the air is smoke-free.

The church has become a Sunday routine for many Christians proclaiming to be saved. Society has put the church on the map as a popular place to go broken and leave broke. How has the church gone from being a soul-saving business to a place of business?

Just when you think you found a man of God to watch over your soul, the detector goes off. He's married with children outside of his marriage and still fooling around. Churches are tolerating the deacons stealing money and flirting with all the single young women—another false alarm. You have members and musicians out at the club on Saturday night—more smoke in the air. We're playing with no anointing, singing with no power, and preaching with no conviction. All the things we're doing is leaving smoke in the air and smuggling our fire.

In any other house, you would pray for no fire, but in God's house, we should be praying for fire. Not the fire with flames, but the Holy Ghost fire, the fire that destroys yokes and sets captives free. We need the fire experience talked about in Acts, the one accord experience. In Hebrews 12:29, we read that "God is a consuming fire." How do we expect God to move in an atmosphere that the fullness of His presence doesn't dwell?

We have not only allowed Satan to get an assigned seat at the church. Now he is the master of ceremonies! Our minds are on everything except the Word of God. All the pastor has to do is holler, and you leave church talking about how you felt the Spirit of the Lord! People aren't trying to live right anymore. With Satan running the service, you get just what he wants you to get: nothing. You should be fed up with just going to church and not getting anything out of it, and you're putting in an offering and investing your time there weekly. We can't allow Satan to play us to where we feel okay with going in the world, doing any and everything that the world does and as long as we're in church on Sunday we are ok. God isn't pleased!

Bringing the world's deceitful ways in God's house, this isn't acceptable. Young people, if you don't want to work, the Bible says you don't eat. If you can't stay out of bars and clubs, you need to stay out of the choir and off the instruments. Ushers that have bad attitudes need to be ushered to a seat. Stop allowing this nonsense in the house of God. We need to put our focus back on the church, which is God's business. Once we take care of God's business, everything else will line up.

Satan has performed many spiritual abortions, snatching the life right out of God's children. He has stolen our joy, peace of mind, and happiness. Now we don't have authority over the devil or the will to fight because we don't have any fire. Young people, put your robe on, and stop being raped by the devil. We are a royal priesthood. Stop being fooled by Satan's smoke bombs. If you're going to be effective and used in the kingdom, you have to align your life up with the Word of God. If your house isn't covered by the blood of Jesus, now would be a good time to have Him stop by, inspect your house, and ignite your fire.

Corrective Hearing, Vision Impaired, Get Your Mind Right

You might be thinking something doesn't look right. You might be saying to yourself that this is mixed up and out of order. Nowadays, mixed up and out of order is becoming more and more popular. The world is confused, and the church is no longer the example for living right. What God is doing now is the same thing that car companies have to do every once in a while—they put out a recall on certain parts.

It's a GMC (God-manufactured Christians) recall. He builds us for heavy weights, to go for miles, to be durable and yet comfortable in the inside. We are built to be the finest on the streets, but yet some of His products get out there, and now they are falling apart. Some God-manufactured Christians are breaking down, and roadside assistance isn't enough. God needs to take some people back to the factory and rebuild them again with all-new parts.

The engine, which is the mind of the vehicle, is one of the first parts that should be rebuilt. Some of us need to get our minds right. We can feel Him pushing our control buttons; instead, we use our own GPS (getting played by sin) system, which leads down the road of destruction every time. A lot of our batteries are out of juice. We need to be recharged daily, constantly needing a jump to get back on the road. With some folks, as soon as they start their engine in the morning, all you here is their muffler (mouth) over every other noise! Some people just need it repaired with the Jesus touch, not Midas! Others need oil changes and refilled or topped off because there is a leak somewhere in their prayer line.

God can't allow backyard mechanics working on us or take the chance of His products trying to fix their problems themselves. He must do all the repairs. God can't fix your ride through life unless you can detect that it's not a smooth ride and a lot is going on under the hood. You need a tune-up, so take it to Jesus. If you're honest with yourself you will admit that sometimes it's hard to see or hear how jacked up you are! Some can't see where they're headed because it's a crack in the windshield blocking their visablilty, while others need to stay off the streets because they have poor vision.

We should all keep the renew solution handy not just for the contacts we wear in our eyes but also for spiritual contacts with God. This solution will remind us God can renew us, and we need to renew our minds daily. Instead of corrective vision, we need our hearing evaluated. Impaired is how doctors would diagnose our hearing. I see our vision as being impaired or diminishing. We've become blindsided to the roadblocks and signs of the times. Flashing red lights aren't even making us stop living in sin. People don't have the fear of God in them anymore; we no longer honor God for who He is.

A friend and I were talking about how we have been in church all our lives, and it appears like we were always struggling. Other people that we knew didn't go or half went to church were at the club every week, drinking, smoking, and doing whatever else they wanted to do, they had nice homes, cars and good jobs. We would hear them talking in one breath how the Lord blessed them, and in the other breath how they got drunk at the bar.

One thing I had to learn was many people are being deceived and will be detoured because they base everything off material things, the things they can see. God is the source of our blessings, but don't be confused—Satan blesses his children too. The Bible says, "Now we know that God heareth not sinners: but if a man be a worshipper of God, and doeth His will, him He heareth" (John 9:31). Understand that God does hear a heart of repentance and has mercy on whom He wishes. You have to look at the full view, not just the side- and rearview mirrors when serving God. Satan knows that some people are so materialistic that all he has to do is keep giving them material things.

God is the gas that will keep you going. He is waiting on you to exhaust all your other options so He can show you who has always been in control of the wheel! Deuteronomy 26 talks about all the blessings of obedience and curses for disobedience. Some of us are going to church week after week and are still not hearing correctly. We hear what we want, which makes it so easy to do what we want. You will never hear from God if you're at a church that is worldly and full of flesh.

Some people are in need of hearing aids because they can't hear the truth. This generation of young people wants to go back on the road without being totally assembled. After hearing a few sermons on how to be blessed, they are ready to roll. Young folks are driving everyone crazy, having deaf ears on the sermons that doesn't agree with their ungodly behavior because they think they have a little polish about themselves.

Chances are when you don't hear right, you can't live right. We know that confusion isn't of God, if you're living confused by not hearing correctly or if your vision is impaired, then you need to find your way back to the shop (church) because that is the key to starting your ignition for Christ and being part of a body that is built to last!

CHAPTER 11

Graduation Day

Many people look at death as a scary part of life. I have discovered that if you lived according to God's Word, then it doesn't have to be a scary experience. When I lost people in my life, with my carnal way of thinking, I'd say, "I won't be able to make it." But once I became spiritual, I viewed death a little differently. I learned that to be absent from the body is to be present with the Lord; if you're ready when He returns, the dead in Christ will rise first. While we're saying they're dead, I say that's wrong because you don't start really living until you die in Christ. Death for the Christian is a promotion to the highest degree, but for the Sinner it's a demotion to the hottest degree!

Lights Out, Time to Go

I would like to take you on a journey through the life of what you might call an ordinary girl, but I called an angel. Before she was conceived, she was special. Her mother was baptized while she carried her in the womb. This young girl was called the speaking-in-tongues baby, later named Dionne Denise by her older sister. At a young age, she was always attached to her mother, making it hard for her to go to preschool. Growing up just a little, she was able to start school because she had her big sister near. Throughout her journey in life, she excelled in all she did.

Her outgoing personality sparked her interest in various clubs. Dionne became a member of student council and the law club, she was her senior class treasurer, president of Jobs Program, she was part of National Honor Society, *Who's Who among American High School Students*, a young American scholar, and she even participated in varsity sports. Dionne's senior year in high school, she was crowned homecoming queen, and graduated in the top ten of her class. It seems as if it would have been almost impossible to live a life so perfect.

After excelling in grade, middle, and high school, she later tested herself on a higher level and enrolled in Ohio State, double majoring in four years. Dionne married a young man, and before becoming parents to their own children, Dionne thought it would be good if they could share their world with kids who were less fortunate. They decided to become foster parents to teenage boys. They had about eleven boys in their home over the course of five years, until they felt it was time to pursue their own family. She was reluctant to have kids because of the thoughts of not being around to watch them grow up. This was something she figured the devil had put in her head when she was a young girl. She later found out that the devil isn't the only one who can say things we don't like, but sometimes God tells us things to prepare us to accept His eternal will.

She later gave birth to two boys, Andre Jr. and Amir. Wanting to carry out the dreams God placed in her heart regarding her two boys, Dionne and her husband decided to move so they could pursue a career in modeling for their oldest child. They were preparing to move to California.

Their family first left Columbus, Ohio, and moved to Akron, Ohio, where they were going to stay for only a short while, so they thought. Dionne began doing what she loved, working with kids until she became ill. At the age of twenty-eight, Dionne developed an ear infection that would not heal. After being tested over a period of six months, she soon discovered she had developed a disease called leukemia. With friends and loved ones on her side, and an excellent medical staff, Dionne had to battle more than just cancer; she was now faced with life-changing decisions regarding her babies. She had to overcome her personal fears of not wanting kids because of this reason, not being able to watch them grow up.

Dionne was a disciple for God, and her missionary work never ended. Enduring blood clots in both legs, her heart stopping, going into a coma, she still managed not to complain, but in all things, she directed all her energy towards praise and worship. She had a bone marrow transplant, which was a perfect match from her oldest sister. It was a successful procedure with unsuccessful end results. Dionne found out on her last day that it didn't take, which resulted in her doctor giving up on her. Dionne's cancer soon returned, and she developed a tumor on her spine, which took Dionne's ability to walk. Still faithful, she witnessed to others of the goodness and mercies of God.

During her experience with cancer, the Lord kept her in perfect peace. He assured her of everlasting comfort in a dream that increased her faith. The Lord had prepared her for every battle she had to fight. Turning her will over to God's will, she accepted God's offer and went through the open door. God was Dionne's door.

You might be wondering who this girl is and what her life has to do with yours. This young lady of honor was my sister. I thought her life would be an inspiration to someone who says, "I am young, I have a little while to get it together." No man knows the day or the hour of God's return. If you're sixteen, you say, "I'll wait until I'm twenty-one." When you're twenty-one, you say you'll wait until you mature a little bit, till you're twenty-five. When you're twenty-five, you say you'll wait until you're thirty, thinking by then you'll be ready to settle down and live right. The devil is going to always have your timing off. What if Dionne would have said she would wait until she was thirty? Guess what? She would not have made it; she died at the age of twenty-nine!

We must stop putting things off for tomorrow. Like many young adults, we have all the answers to life. Nobody knows more than us, and that's why so many of our youth can go to church week after week and still play with God. I found out how short and final life really is when I watched my sister lying in that hospital bed day after day with so much courage. She had to know in her heart she would never see her sons grow up, never get to spend another anniversary with the man she loved, never get to talk to her best friend again, never get to see her siblings' kids grow up, get married, and have their families. Everything in this world was vanishing right before her eyes, and there wasn't anything or anyone that could change the will of God.

At funerals, you hear over and over, "They're going home to be with the Lord." Everyone isn't going to be with the Lord! Revelation 20:15 says, "And whosoever was not found written in the book of life was cast into the lake of fire." Everyone believes for some reason they are going to heaven. What separates your life from the sinners if you're talking, dressing, and carrying on like the world? It's time out acting like you don't know what God requires of you. The Bible tells us that "except a man be born again, he cannot see the kingdom of God" (John 3:3). We are cautioned not to be just hearers of the Word but doers, for God informs us we're only deceiving ourselves. Stop saying you don't need to go to church because you and God have your own understanding...your deceiving yourself! You need a watchman over your soul. The Bible says for us not to forsake the assembling of ourselves together (Heb.10:25).

When I watched her witness in spite of her circumstances, Dionne proved that even though she was immobile physically, she could still walk the walk spiritually. Before my sister passed, she told me that when she got better, the two of us would go all over the world with her testimony, and today I feel she is all better, and her testimony is being fulfilled through me.

I challenge young people around the world to come out from among them and live for God. You don't have as much time as you think. God wishes that none of his children perish. He's calling many, but your lifestyles will be the determining factor if you're chosen! The same way you would ensure you had all your credits to graduate in the natural you need to check your list in the spiritual. Are you saved, filled with the spirit of God, have you been baptized, and living holy? If you answered "YES" to all the questions you have all your credits to move up to the next level. If you answered "NO" than you better use your time wisely and prepare for your big day. God says, "Surely, I come quickly." On graduation, I hope you hear "Good job, my good and faithful servant" and not "Depart from me, I never knew you!" Ready or not, it will be lights out and time to go. Heaven and hell is real! Youth Better Reckon-Eyes!

AUTHOR'S NOTE

Since I can remember how to coo, crawl, or walk, I was in church. When I was a little girl, I have always had a desire to go to church and pay my tithes and offerings out of my lunch money. I have always loved and had a passion to serve God. When I didn't live up to the Word of God, I still knew I was special in God's sight. I always knew that the Lord wanted great things for me.

Once I graduated from school, I began to get back on track and began to want more out of life than what I was getting. I began to pray and fast, asking the Lord what I needed to do to get out of the repeated cycles I was experiencing. The more I said yes to the Lord and the more I surrendered my own will, that's when I began to see manifestations of my visions and dreams. I ran into many detours with people, jobs, and even deaths. Throughout it all God, showed His faithfulness.

As I started to look around the church, I could not believe that it had become so money-oriented and hip-hop cultured, and there were so many church atmospheres that weren't anointed. Because I hungered for young people to know what Christ really would do for them, I started asking the Lord to help me to minister to other young people in a different way. I had a desire to be used by God in a mighty way. I knew once I lined up with His will, what God had for me to do would shake the nations. I began taking necessary steps to getting pregnant. After graduating and moving to Detroit, Michigan, I didn't know that this would be the place of conception for me. This was where the seed of salvation was dropped into my spirit; I got saved and filled with the Holy Ghost here.

While seeing that I was getting bigger, as the dream grew, I began to get scared, like most pregnant girls. Running from my problems that followed me because it was part of me, I ended up in Georgia. Here was the place where I felt labor pains like never before. This was the place where I stayed on my face before the Lord, sowing and giving all of me in every way. I turned my cousin Arthaniel's home into my hospital room, or you can call it my sanctuary. I felt every kick, and because I was in unfamiliar territory, it became very uncomfortable.

As time progressed, I ended up back in Ohio because my sister became very ill. Not even a year later, I lost her. I began to write and seek God with all I had, and I diligently began walking in His will. Being touched by so many special doctors and nurses while my sister was in the hospital, I knew that my purpose for being there was much deeper than just taking care of my sister. God allowed me to witness and to display His peace. He showed many people how He would keep your mind in the midst of the storm.

Even after this trying situation, I began to push through the pains, out of my pain, and I finally gave birth to the dream God had planted on the inside, *Youth Better Reckon-Eyes*! This was a part of my spiritual walk that tested me in the fire, and I hope that this book shows the world how God can and will bring you out as gold. God bless you.

Printed in the United States
By Bookmasters